JONNY MAGIC AND THE CARD SHARK KIDS

How a Gang of Geeks Beat the Odds and Stormed Las Vegas

DAVID KUSHNER

KT-164-277

WILLIAM HEINEMANN: LONDON

Published in the United Kingdom by William Heinemann, 2006

1 3 5 7 9 10 8 6 4 2

Copyright © David Kushner, 2006

David Kushner has asserted his right under the Copyright, Designs and Patents Act, 1988 to be identified as the author of this work.

First published in the United States by Random House, an imprint of the Random House Publishing Group, a division of Random House Inc., New York.

William Heinemann
The Random House Group Limited
20 Vauxhall Bridge Road, London, SW1V 2SA

Random House Australia (Pty) Limited
20 Alfred Street, Milsons Point, Sydney
New South Wales 2061, Australia

Random House New Zealand Limited
18 Poland Road, Glenfield
Auckland 10, New Zealand

Random House (Pty) Limited
Isle of Houghton, Corner of Boundary Road & Carse O'Gowrie, Houghton
2198, South Africa

The Random House Group Limited Reg. No. 954009

www.randomhouse.co.uk

A CIP catalogue record for this book is available from the British Library
Papers used by Random House are natural, recyclable products made from wood grown in sustainable forests. The manufacturing processes conform to the environmental regulations of the country of origin

ISBN 0 4340 16071

Printed and bound in Great Britain by
Clays Ltd, St Ives Plc

For my parents

CONTENTS

PRELUDE: THE NEW HIGH ROLLERS *ix*

1. DAWN OF THE DORK *3*
2. GEEK POKER *13*
3. THE MAGIC BULLET *21*
4. JERSEY KIDS VS. DEAD GUYS *37*
5. FINKELTRON *55*
6. ROUNDERS *71*
7. JONNY MAGIC *91*
8. THE CARD SHARK KIDS *113*
9. SEND IN THE CLOWNS *135*
10. ALL-IN *151*
11. THE FINAL TABLE *159*
12. THE ONLY GAME IN TOWN *173*

EPILOGUE *179*

APPENDIX A: MAGIC: THE GATHERING BASICS *185*

APPENDIX B: TEXAS HOLD 'EM POKER BASICS *189*

APPENDIX C: BLACKJACK BASICS *193*

GLOSSARY *199*

NOTES *207*

BIBLIOGRAPHY *211*

AUTHOR'S NOTE *215*

ACKNOWLEDGMENTS *219*

PRELUDE

The New High Rollers

The card shark kids shot from their mansion over the neon streets of Vegas. It was time to take down another game and, today, it was the big one.

In the pulsating heart of the Glitter Gulch—the canopied mall of casinos downtown—sheiks and freaks, boxers and brokers, movie stars and soccer moms, playmates and jailbait swarmed under the flashing red marquee of Binion's Horseshoe for the 2004 World Series of Poker.

Every year since 1970, poker nuts from around the planet descended upon the Horseshoe to compete for the ultimate bounty: the diamond-encrusted championship bracelet and multimillion-dollar cash prize. This year, with a record $20 million on the table, the stakes were juicier than ever.

Poker was in renaissance. Long relegated to hustlers and cowboys, the game had erupted into a mainstream obsession. It started the previous year, when the Travel Channel began beaming the World Poker Tour into homes. Then a restaurant accountant named Chris Moneymaker came from seemingly nowhere to win $2.5 million—a Cinderella story broadcast repeatedly on ESPN. Armchair gamblers imagined rising from their living-room games to become the next champ. Online gambling exploded. Vegas boomed. Winning millions at the World Series of Poker, long the biggest game in town, became an international dream.

Today, 2,576 players, three times as many as in 2003, had anted up to $10,000 to take a seat inside the legendary Horseshoe. One after the other, the big shots arrived. Ben Affleck, Hollywood's poker poster boy, flashed incandescently through the crowd. Doyle Brunson, the towering seventy-one-year-old World Series veteran, hobbled in to a burst of applause. No one expected a gang of geeks to crush them at their own game. But that's just what the young guys heading unnoticed inside were about to do.

By the end of the tournament, the card shark kids would take the final tables for more than $4 million. It wasn't a lucky streak; it was an infiltration. Reporters gawked at what they termed the "army of young amateurs" and "year of the young guns." As one of the sharks said, "This is our Normandy." But for their hero, Jon Finkel, a lanky twenty-six-year-old in a Battle School hooded sweatshirt and backward Phillies baseball cap, it was kid's stuff.

Unlike professional gamblers who specialize in one area of action, Finkel had become a self-made millionaire by storming the gaming world on all fronts. He razed underground poker clubs and online sites. He rose to the top of the country's largest card-counting blackjack team, earning a place on the most-wanted list of nearly every casino around. Lately he was conquering the most seemingly unbeatable game of all, sports betting.

And he wasn't alone. Unbeknownst to the old guard at the Horseshoe, Finkel's friends had also been raking in cash before they could legally set foot inside a casino, or see an R-rated movie. They'd been card sharks since their early teens. What's even more remarkable is how these misfit brainiacs found each other, and their winning edge.

Their secret is Magic.

Magic: The Gathering is a card game that has quietly spawned an international phenomenon and multibillion-dollar industry. Brought to market in 1993 for under $100,000, it outsells Monopoly and Scrabble combined. It is overlooked, misunderstood, and, for some of the smartest young people on the planet, profoundly influential. Those who seek insight into the future of Wall Street traders, research scientists, poker stars, technologists, and boot-strapped entrepreneurs would be well served to sit down at a neighborhood Magic game.

Created by an iconoclastic, Ivy League mathematician named Dr. Richard Garfield, Magic combines mythological fantasy, baseball card–style collectibility, and raw competitive strategy into something unique: it's called a trading card game. The fundamental design, which Garfield patented, is the basis of cottage industry titles such as Pokemon and Yu-Gi-Oh! It's also the reason Hasbro—the powerhouse behind Playskool, Tonka, and Milton Bradley toys and games—paid a half billion bucks to buy Wizards of the Coast, the scrappy start-up Garfield co-owned. The trail of Magic's shiny wrappers runs through pizza joints and dorm rooms, summer camps and cafeterias from the Main Streets of New Jersey to the alleys of Japan. The game, published in ten languages and fifty-two countries, is now Hasbro's top brand.

For the best players, it's also a lucrative lifestyle. Starting as young as fourteen, the elite travel to exotic locales from Rio de Janeiro to Kuala Lumpur competing in tournaments for $3 million in cash prizes. The pros make a living at Magic alone. With individual earnings as high as $350,000, many have put themselves through college with the game. In short, Magic is transforming legions of neglected whiz kids into ultra-savvy teenage high rollers or, as Garfield likes to call them, "mental athletes." Now this new generation of players—

weaned on video games, schooled on Magic, and empowered by the Internet—is coming of age and cashing in.

But their rise has not come without controversy. Magic has been banned by schools, counterfeited by crooks, blamed for Satanism, thievery, and ritual death. It has been called evil, blasphemous, and "cardboard crack." With more Magic veterans popping up at poker tables, the game is becoming causally linked with the surge in teenage gambling. Parents and pundits want to know why their brightest young bulbs are dropping out of college and forgoing prestigious careers for this. "We could be finding the cure for cancer, but instead we're playing cards," Finkel says. "Why is that?"

Finkel's story provides an answer. For millions of fans, his remarkable transformation from chump to champ is already the inspirational stuff of legend. He's the Rocky of playing cards: a sympathetic underdog who, through skill and determination, beat enormous odds to become a World Champion. Beaten up by jocks, overlooked by teachers, and shunned by girls, he was once an overweight, suicidal, self-described "loser" who typified how smart, awkward boys in America get lost in the shuffle. Now this slim and confident millionaire epitomizes how, in the most unlikely ways, they're being found.

"It's amazing that a guy like me can become the best in the world at something," he says. And once you find your edge, he knows, there's nothing you can't do.

Inside the Horseshoe, the players took their seats. Cameras rolled. Chips stacked. Finkel reached for his cards. Big players have nicknames, and it was time for the world to learn his. The geeks used to call him Finkeltron. Today they call him Jonny Magic.

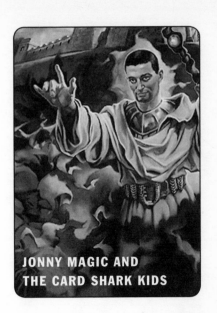

JONNY MAGIC AND
THE CARD SHARK KIDS

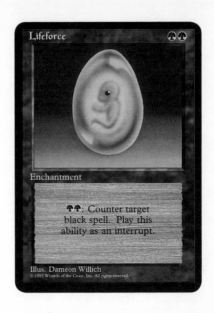

1. DAWN OF THE DORK

"Yo no soy marinero! Yo no soy marinero! Soy capitan! Soy capitan!
Soy capitan! Bamba bamba! Bamba bamba! Bamba bamba!"

Fourteen-year-old Jon Finkel rocked inside his Lilliputian chair in
the back of the classroom, singing at the top of his lungs. As his
gelatinous body swayed, his bottom roll of stomach fat bulged under
the desk's Juicy Fruit stalactites. A black stained Phillies T-shirt
flapped over his loose jeans. His long tangled hair curled like a roller
coaster into what he affectionately termed his "Jewfro." An enormous pair of square glasses slipped down a long, large nose that bent
in the middle like it was perpetually ducking a punch. His eyes were
two frantic bugs sealed in novelty ice cubes.

As he hit the last note of the song, he pushed his glasses back into
place and raised his flabby arms in the air with a triumphant "Hey!"

But no applause came. This wasn't music class. It was geography. And by the looks of the bored, pencil-chewing students around him, this strange and unprovoked burst of song was nothing unusual. Finkel, the biggest loser in school, was just being Finkel again.

In the social hierarchy of eighth grade at Park Middle School in Fanwood, New Jersey, in 1992, Finkel was anything but a high roller. Here, as in most schools, there were two ways for a boy to be an outcast. You could be smart. Or you could be weird. If you were dumb and normal, that was fine, particularly if you could hit a ball far with a stick. Finkel embodied the worst of both worlds: he was both smart and weird.

Naturally, the kids hated him.

Finkel's unique and stubborn smarts ran in the family. His dad, Mark, a computer analyst, was a headstrong and liberal math nerd who made a career out of speaking his mind. While working as a cryptographer for the National Security Agency, he spoke out loudly against the Vietnam war. When he lost his security clearance for smoking pot, he got drafted—only to declare himself a conscientious objector.

While working as a VISTA volunteer, a community service group, in Brockport, New York, Mark met Claire Byrne, an elementary school teacher who had dropped out of a different institution: the convent. After six years studying to be a nun, Claire decided her faith wasn't strong enough to inspire a lifetime vow. She wanted something new. She found it in Mark, an argumentative Jew from Philadelphia. The two married, and two days after their first child was born on May 18, 1978, Claire and the boy converted to Judaism.

After moving to New Jersey, where Mark got a job as a computer analyst with the British Oxygen Company, the Finkels nurtured the exceptional intellects of Jon and his new baby sister, Jenny. When Jon was four, his father taught him to convert numbers into binary code. It became something of a parlor trick.

"Hey Jon, what's twelve in binary?" his dad would ask on the fly.

"1100!" the curly-haired boy replied.

To improve Jon's math skills, Mark programmed a computer

game called Hex Baseball; for the characters to advance, Jon had to correctly answer hexadecimal arithmetic questions. To teach his son to read, Mark designed a modification of a computer game called Colossal Cave Adventure. Every time Jon typed in a directional command—Go, Turn Left—the character on the screen responded accordingly. At bedtime, Mark didn't read to Jon from *Hop on Pop,* but from his dog-eared collection of science fiction and fantasy novels. The boy would fall asleep dreaming of shiny spaceships and green-skinned Orcs.

By the time he got to kindergarten, Jon's exceptional nature and nurture were readily apparent. "He's not only reading," his teacher effused, "he's reading at a third-grade level!" Before long, Finkel was reading his dad's books by himself. One time, after reading his son nightly chapters of *The Fellowship of the Ring,* Mark had to go away on a business trip. When he came back two days later, he picked the book back up, but there was no need. Jon had read two hundred pages ahead on his own. He was seven.

The other side of his brain continued blooming, too. One afternoon, Claire brought him to nearby Kean College, where she was getting a degree in math. Inside a physics classroom, a professor noticed the pudgy boy fidgeting with a ruler. For fun, he asked the boy to compare two measurements. When Finkel quickly calculated the difference in length, the teacher arched his brow. "You should send him to private school," he told Claire.

Hoping to provide their son with a greater range of experience, however, Finkel's parents stuck with public school. They knew their boy was different, but, as Claire said, she wanted him to be "normal." Yet there was nothing normal about him. After finishing his classwork early, Finkel would waddle to his teacher's desk to hand in his work. Along the way, he would tell each student he passed all the wrong stuff they had written down on their papers. To make matters worse, Jon had developed a loud and fast manner of speaking, similar to his mother's. In his mind, he was just pointing out the obvious, but as far as other kids were concerned, Finkel was just being a jerk. And they would make him pay.

The taunts came early: "Jon Jon leprechaun, went to school with nothing on, teacher told him what to wear, polka-dotted underwear." Boys are defined by whatever rhymes with their last names. Some names insulate them from pain. Others invite it. "Finkel," as Jon quickly learned, was a death sentence. His name rhymed with Wrinkle, like the pale rolls of baby fat on his adolescent belly. It rhymed with Stinkel—not even a real word, but a stigma nonetheless, a condemnation: Finkel, he who stinks. And, as they showed him one day, it rhymed with Tinkle, too.

After school, Finkel was walking home when a gang of bullies burst after him. Too slow and heavy to outrun them, Finkel got cornered. The next thing he knew, he was on the ground. Someone's fly unzipped, and warm awful liquid rained down. The bullies left him there dripping in a hapless wet pile. If schools are divided into jocks and nerds, then Finkel had just been drafted as the biggest loser for the losing team.

"Harrrrggggggggggggggghhhhhhhhhhhhhhhhhhhh!" came the horrific hurling sound from behind the bathroom door. The groan climaxed with a titanic splash. Then it ceased. Silence. Faint gulping of air. And then, again, terribly, the tidal wave recommenced, this time more horrifically fluid than before, a class-six white-water rapid of insides slamming into a porcelain vortex.

Leaning casually against the wall, Finkel stifled a yawn and checked his watch. Then he growled dramatically again. Reaching up high above his head, he poured a bucket of water down into the bowl. Rather than deal with the pain of school, Finkel played sick. But this game required skill. He had to be convincing, subtle. He didn't want to come on too strong. He had to splash just enough liquid in the bowl to arouse compassion. It required analysis, cunning, an ability to size up the moment, to read the barometer of a parent's sympathy meter. Some mornings, all it took to convince his parents was a bit of wailing in bed. Other mornings, such as today, he had to employ the water buckets. He splashed one more bit into the bowl, before concluding with a flush, and a yelp.

For a while, the sick game worked. He spent his days ensconced in his room, devouring books of fantasy and science fiction. Before long, he was up to five books a week. He stormed through all his dad's dusty classics: Heinlein, Asimov, Bradbury. And he discovered what would become his own personal bible: *Ender's Game* by Orson Scott Card. The book detailed the futuristic adventures of Ender Wiggin, a boy genius drafted by the military at age six to save the world from an alien invasion. A master of war games, Ender quickly rises to the top of the army's so-called Battle School—only to discover the price, and pain, of his gift. Finkel could relate.

After one too many water symphonies in the bathroom, his parents knew something serious was paining their gifted son. Though Finkel didn't talk about it, he obviously dreaded going to school. He had no friends. And while his younger sister, Jenny, also smart, was acting like a social butterfly, Jon just seemed to be digging farther into his cocoon.

Soon enough, the truth came out. During parent conferences, his teachers complained about Jon's confrontational attitude. They also mentioned how he was being bullied for acting so smart in front of the other kids. Though Claire and Mark didn't know the extent of the beatings, it was enough to rend their hearts. "Jon's intellectually ahead, but emotionally behind," Mark said. "The combination of the two is deadly." Claire agreed. "Once you get labeled a victim," Mark said, "it builds upon itself." Something had to be done.

Since Mark and Claire were both self-ordained smart weirdos in their day, they pleaded with Jon to keep a low profile.

"Don't raise your hand every time you know the answer," Mark said.

"You can't go down the aisle in class telling the kids how smart you are," Claire said. "They resent it."

"When you do good on a test," Mark added, "keep your mouth shut."

Jon lowered his head and nodded quietly.

"When you get older," Claire said, reassuringly, "you'll see, things will get better." But, deep inside, she hated the hypocrisy of that sentiment. The football games were on the front page of the local paper; the chess club was on page sixteen. Why was it that a boy could boast of his physical prowess but not his mental abilities? If a boy wants to trash-talk, then there's an accepted place to do that: on the playing field. So that's where Finkel went.

Though Finkel was nerdy, that didn't mean he was uninterested in sports. He was an Eagles and Phillies fanatic. On weekends, he'd watch all the games with his dad, devouring every statistic on every player on the teams. Noticing his increasing weight, his dad encouraged Jon to get involved in playing sports on his own. Finkel squeezed into a soccer uniform and proceeded to embarrass himself on the field.

He told his parents he wanted to try another sport, like baseball. Mark wanted him to stick with the existing game. But the boy was adamant.

"Dad," he said, earnestly, "every kid wants to be a baseball hero."

Finkel joined the team. Not long after he started, he got hit in the head with a baseball and spent the rest of the year on the bench. But he never lost his passion to compete. He was just as strong as, if not stronger than, any other boy. It was just that his strength wasn't in his arms or legs, but in his brain. Why should that make him any less of an athlete? Why should that make him any less of an all-American boy? If he couldn't be an athlete in body, why not, then, in mind?

But no one ever became Randall Cunningham with just a brain. Sure, Finkel was the first kid in his bar mitzvah class to learn his Haftorah, but how many girls would daydream about that? Aside from the school quiz bowl team, which he led, Finkel had nowhere else to compete, nowhere to shine. Without an outlet, he expressed himself like generations of smart and persecuted American boys had done before.

Finkel got weird.

It was ten minutes before he had to leave for school, and Finkel checked himself over in the bathroom mirror. His hair twisted in Cubist mats of knots. His black T-shirt and baggy pants congealed with stains. The rising smell seemed to seal him in a dreadful green womb. If everyone thinks I'm a big freak, then, screw it, he decided, that's what I'm going to be; I can play this game, too. He wasn't faking sick this morning, he was going to school.

By the time he turned fourteen, Finkel had hardened into the unrelentingly geeky loser everyone had made him out to be. He stopped combing his hair. He stopped showering as often. He picked his nose acrobatically in front of other kids. And, though he was raised kosher, he stopped caring about what he ate. At lunch, he would gorge on McDonald's. At home, he would sneak into the bathroom after dessert and devour Fruit Roll-Ups.

At school, he lumbered down the halls like a big greasy mess of angry fat dork meat. Still the smartest kid in school, he chucked his mom's advice out the window and began brandishing his brain power at every opportunity. When he realized a group of kids were copying off him during a test, he purposely wrote down the wrong answers—sacrificing his own score just to keep them from doing well.

He showed up the teachers, too. Once, an instructor was insisting that Mount Washington was in upstate New York. Finkel knew she was wrong, because his dad had gone hiking on that mountain on a vacation. "You're completely wrong!" he said, hoisting his arm in the air. "Mount Washington's in New Hampshire."

"No," the teacher said, "it's in New York."

"No," Finkel said, more loudly, "it's in New! Hampshire!"

When she ignored him, he broke into an impromptu performance of "La Bamba." It felt like the right thing to do.

Fed on a steady diet of science fiction and junk food, Finkel became a powerhouse geek. But that didn't mean he identified with his peers. At this point, years before the dot-com boom of the late 1990s, brainy boys weren't icons of millionaire chic. They weren't geeks, they were just nerds. And there was a big difference between the two.

At school, Finkel discovered, the nerds had their own petty little social structure. He called it the Nerd Pyramid. As a subset of the school's larger ecosystem, the Nerd Pyramid housed all the pariahs.

And the boys inside it could be as brutally competitive as the jocks. Finkel got into loud, argumentative matches with the other kids, trying to argue, say, why time travel is scientifically plausible. He argued so much, and so well, his parents thought he should become a lawyer. Finkel told them he was going to go to Princeton to become a genetic researcher. But, in reality, he had other ideas; he just didn't know what they were yet.

No matter how much he rebelled and postured, Finkel couldn't find his edge. The beatings continued—before school, after school, during school. The bullies grew so tired of beating him up that they had to invent new ways to keep it interesting. One time, they said they were going to beat him until he laughed; and they did, socking away at his ribs until he complied with a fake hearty chuckle.

But the worst came one day when the entire student population was gathered in the gymnasium. Just before the event, a swarm of bullies closed in on Finkel. And within seconds, the fists and kicks followed. Stinkel curled on the floor while a crowd of students watched his anguish. When he squinted through his tears, he saw that it wasn't just the lunkhead mutants unleashing the blows, it was the all-American boys: the perfect blond-haired, blue-eyed athletes the parents and newspapers adored.

No one wants to believe that the nice, good-looking, popular boys are the bullies, Finkel realized, but that's exactly who they are! It's the smart kid who is at the bottom of the pile. What kind of upside-down fantasy world is this? It's the law of science fiction: no matter how twisted a world seems, it has its own set of laws, its source of balance. If the smart kid was at the bottom of the pile, maybe there was something that could bring him to the top.

The news couldn't have come at a better time: the Finkels were moving to England. Jon's dad, who had been working at the New Jersey office of the British Oxygen Company, got an offer to transfer to the company's office in Woking, a town thirty-seven miles southwest of London. The pay would be good. The kids would go to a fancy, international private school. And the family would be put in a big house with a luxury car. With Jon seemingly more and more despondent, his heartsick parents welcomed the change. So did their son. Bring it on! he said. He didn't have any friends anyway, so there was no one to leave behind. With a fresh start, life could only get better, he figured.

He was wrong. It was fall 1993; Finkel was fifteen. It took only days at his new school in England for the old patterns to begin. Though he was dressed in the uniform of a jacket, tie, and turtleneck, Finkel's fat face, square glasses, and nest of kinky hair was as big a nerd siren as before. Kids laughed, poked, and teased. No matter where I go in the world, he thought, I'll be mocked. Finkel hunched over his desk and scrawled onto his notebook the headline: "10 Reasons to Not Commit Suicide."

One day after school, he threw the notebook in his backpack, hopped on his bike, and pedaled through the gray streets of Woking, trying in vain to think of reasons for his list. This time, however, the answers didn't come easy. His big burly analytical brain ruthlessly sought the meaning of his life.

For years, his parents had encouraged him to think for himself. And now, miles from nowhere, zooming through ugly streets, he thought for himself once and for all: everything his parents told him, he realized, was a lie. They said life would get better when he got older, that kids wouldn't pick on him like before. But they were wrong. They had fed him religion, another lie. The only reason he was a Jew, he thought, was because his parents were Jews; if they had raised him a Christian, then that's what he'd be. Religion wasn't a fact, it was a matter of opinion. It was make believe. There was no afterlife. Though he read fantasy, he couldn't believe in magic. He was sure it couldn't exist.

Emerging from the ether of his thoughts, Finkel found himself rolling slowly by a store called Fun and Games. He had passed the shop before but had never taken notice. This time, he stopped his bike, propped it against the wall, and went inside. It felt like he had entered an architectural realization of his own brain. A papier-mâché dragon hung from the ceiling. Posters of wizards and warriors covered the walls. Steely miniature trolls lined the shelves. Around a junk food—strewn table, a group of nerdy guys played cards.

Behind the counter was the owner, a burly man in his thirties with long dark hair and a black leather motorcycle jacket. He took one look at this enormous kid stuffed in a ridiculous turtleneck and blazer, and had just one word to say. It was the most meaningful one Finkel had heard in years: "Welcome!"

Finkel wobbled over to the table. "What's that you're playing?" he asked.

The guy in the motorcycle jacket looked up and grinned. "It's Magic," he said.

As they taught him how to play, it felt as if, for the first time in his life, someone had dealt the cards just for him.

2. GEEK POKER

"Anyone up for some linear algebra?" said Richard Garfield, as he
plucked a fat textbook from the shelf.

It was a warm spring day in 1991 inside the lounge of the David
Rittenhouse Lab, home to the math department at the University of
Pennsylvania in Philadelphia. Garfield, a twenty-eight-year-old Ph.D.
candidate in math, stood with two other graduate students. Wiry and
unshaven, he had jet black aerodynamic hair, a bow tie, and two
different-colored socks. He held the book aloft, eyebrows raised.

"Linear algebra," one of the students said, "yes, let's do some!"

"Linear algebra, indeed!" the other concurred.

Garfield tucked the book under his arm, and the three proceeded
gingerly out the door, passing a professor who waved the intrepid

students enthusiastically on their way. Down the hall, they stepped into an empty classroom with a long green chalkboard of furiously scrawled equations. They shut the door and took their seats. Garfield cracked open the textbook, but there was more than linear algebra inside. The book's pages had been hollowed out to make a secret compartment. Garfield reached inside, and plucked out a deck of playing cards.

It was time for poker.

Ostensibly, for a math student at Penn, poker was more than fun and games. Garfield was studying combinatorics, the science of counting, and poker had more than once been a subject of study. Part of finding the edge in the game is mastering probability: how many possible hands, for example, can be dealt in a game? It is, at its heart, a combinatorial question—one that requires devising a technique for counting.

But for Garfield, games like poker weren't just part of his course of study, they were his course of life. Games are elegant and beautiful mathematical structures, he thought, both an expression of science and an artful means of communication. The classic ones, like chess or Scrabble, pioneered and defined a form; Garfield called these "essence" games. And as he and the math geeks around the department had discovered, few games were more essential than poker.

Poker, Garfield thought, has everything. It can be played for any length of time. Skill is important, but luck clearly matters. In the long term, better players see results, but in the short term, anyone can win. Plus, the game is flexible enough to support modifications—such as Stud, Hold 'Em, or Baseball—that keep players intrigued. Garfield came up with his own poker variants: Zombie, a game that resurrects folded players when a spade ("a shovel, get it?" he'd say) is dealt, and Second Best, where the second-place hand wins. No one liked Second Best, for obvious reasons. But variations, even bad ones, Garfield noted, keep the action interesting.

Back in his bedroom, he considered this as he tinkered away at an original card game of his own, Magic.

. . .

Like Jon Finkel and the generation of card shark kids he would eventually spawn, Garfield was a misfit whiz who tapped the magic power of games early on. One of the first he ever learned was, literally, a matter of life and death. The game was called Hit the Ground. It unfolded, almost daily, at the Garfield home. Out of the blue, one of his parents would yell "Hit the ground!" and Garfield and his two younger sisters would splay themselves on the floor. The first one down won. Garfield, only seven years old, had no idea how high the stakes of the game were.

It was 1970, and his family was living in Bangladesh, where his young father, also named Richard, apprenticed with the internationally renowned architect Louis Kahn. Bangladesh, at the time, roiled in the throes of a bloody revolution. Shots flew regularly outside the Garfield home. A massacre occurred at the university less than a mile down the road. Hit the Ground was actually his parents' way of getting their kids to practice a survival drill. But for little Richard, it was just another game—and a good one at that.

Unable to speak the local language, Garfield, a bright and affable boy, used games as a means of communicating with the neighborhood kids. In Bangladesh, he played marbles in ancient temples. When the family followed Kahn to Nepal, he played tag around ancient ruins. At night, he would lie on the floor and watch his parents play Risk, Monopoly, and cards. Though he couldn't understand the content of their conversations—politics, architecture, cholera—he could follow the rules of the games. And this sense of connection gave him a sense of both comfort and empowerment. Games were a bridge.

Then the bridge collapsed. When he was eleven, Garfield's family moved to Eugene, Oregon, where his father had taken a job at the university. After growing up without television, playing Hit the Ground, and riding elephants, Garfield felt like Tarzan emerging from the jungle. Smart and adventurous, he couldn't find anyone with whom he could relate—until he wandered into a fantasy world that seemed designed for people like him.

Gandalf's Den was a game shop near the University of Oregon.

Posters of dragons lined the purple walls. Psychedelic music played. A closet bulged with weird costumes. Shelves were lined with dusty miniature wizards. In the back, a group of long-haired students in ratty jeans sat around a table throwing a tetrahedral die. One of them had a book cracked open on his lap, and seemed to be telling a story: *You're in the woods, there are large beasts in the shadows, sounds of explosions in the distance . . .*

Garfield blinked. It sounded like familiar territory. He might have been stranded in Oregon, but inside the imaginary world of Dungeons and Dragons, the fantasy game they were playing, he was back home in the jungle again.

Invented in 1972 by a pair of eccentric midwesterners named Gary Gygax and Dave Arneson, D&D, as it became known, was becoming a subcultural phenomenon. In the game, players assume roles such as wizards or warriors, each with his own special abilities. A leader, called the Dungeon Master, or DM, invents a scenario using D&D rule books as a guide. With the players banded together, the DM narrates the adventures through monster-laden forests and caves. When they encounter a beast, the fights are resolved with throws of a multisided die. Unlike most games, the goal isn't to win, but to build character and gain experience from one round to the next.

Garfield was hooked. Gandalf's Den became his community center and library. In addition to playing D&D, he bought or borrowed every genre of game he could find—chess, Go, Scrabble. In his junior high, a progressive school that offered courses on *Star Trek* and plant psychology, Garfield successfully lobbied the school to start a class in the study of games. Already an expert at thirteen, he taught the class himself.

The club attracted a community of like-minded boys: smart, outcast, irreverent. School became one big game board. When another member stole his math textbook and sealed it in duct tape, Garfield retaliated by having his friend's book encased in concrete; the game escalated until Garfield welded a friend's book in an iron box. Later, Garfield orchestrated a sprawling round of Killer, a mock-assassination game that culminated in riddling the unsuspecting homecoming queen with rubber darts.

If any of them had had a shot at dating the queen, of course, they would have chosen a different target. But, as Garfield lamented, this seemed to be their fate. In a perfect world, competitive young brainiacs like him would be respected as much as the baseball team. But they weren't considered mental athletes, they were just thought to be mental. They were denigrated, hung from lockers by their underwear, ridiculed, stomped, and beaten. Their brains made them losers. Real men didn't play Dungeons and Dragons, it seemed. They played poker.

On a clear day in Oregon, Multnomah Falls is a sight to behold. It falls 620 feet in the heart of the lush Columbia River gorge. For some locals, however, it's also a sight to fear. A legend has been passed down over the ages about a young Indian maiden who threw herself off the falls to appease the Great Spirit and save her community from a terrible plague. Some say a visitor could look up into the frothy white mist and see the ghostly maiden staring down from the trees.

But twenty-seven-year-old Garfield, who was hiking up to the falls during one summer vacation from graduate school, wasn't one of them. His father used to take him here as a child and say the cold wind gave him the willies. But Garfield didn't believe in magic. He was a man of science. For him, it was just a waterfall. Today, he had more pressing matters on his mind: selling his first game.

A few days earlier, Garfield had met with an aspiring young game publisher named Peter Adkinson. With a round balding head and cherubic grin, Adkinson was a giddy and impassioned gamer. A Pentecostal preacher's son who, despite accusations of Satanism, became a Dungeons and Dragons fanatic, Adkinson ran his own start-up role-playing game company called Wizards of the Coast, and wanted to expand. "How about coming up with something that's cheap to make and easy to play?" he suggested, something gamers could play in between rounds of D&D. Garfield thought there was nothing faster and cheaper than a card game.

As Garfield passed the trees on the way to the falls, he considered what this game might be. He knew what elements he wanted: something that combined, like poker, a compelling chemistry of luck and skill. All his life, he and his friends lived for that rush of excitement that came with learning a new game; it was a period he defined as "innovation." The rest of game playing is just honing, refining skills. The innovation is the fun part, when anything is possible and anyone, even a loser, can win.

That's why living-room poker players liked the kinetic power of dealer's choice. When they say the one-eyed Jack is wild, they're leveling the field. The reason a card is wild is because it's changing the rules of the game, and the game becomes more alive as a result. Imagine a game, he mused, that imparts a constant sense of adventure and innovation. What if wild is the norm? What if every card breaks the rules? What if innovation is within everyone's grasp?

Dizzy in thought, he suddenly found himself standing at the thunderous foot of Multnomah Falls. A roaring downpour crashed from six stories high into a froth of white foam. It was the middle of summer, but the cold wind blew in full force. That's when the answer hit Garfield. He could see it bursting like a dam, a torrent of playing cards cascading down the mountain and flooding around him.

That's it, he realized, the players have different cards!

It was his first eureka moment, and it was a big one. In most card games, players draw from a communal deck. What if, instead, each player has his or her own deck? And they can build these decks, before the game, from a vast, ever-increasing pool of cards. Each card could have its own magic power!

If I was making chess, Garfield thought, I'd say wow, maybe all these knights should move like rooks, or maybe bombs should be standard, or maybe the board should be shrinking at every turn, there are so many things you can do. But with this kind of game, you can do it all! You can make a card for any wacky thing you can think of and suddenly the game incorporates that into its being. In this new design, you can always be getting new cards to build into your deck and change your game. It would create a constantly changing environment and an unlimited range of possibilities, a state of discovery that is constantly refreshed. It would be alive.

Garfield had already been tinkering around with a card game he called Five Magics. The idea was that players were wizards, dueling each other, and they could draw from cards that represented different spells or creatures. But Garfield had never considered the possibility that the cards could be drawn from an endless pool, that a player could go to a store and plunk down a few bucks and buy a pack of cards, like trading cards, rip open the wrapper, and see what he got. With all his cards spread out in the room, he could assemble his ultimate deck—his magic powers! his creatures! his spells!—and then he could go and play. When he came back, he could buy or trade more cards, and keep building and innovating his deck. Each new card would be new ammunition for the game. It was a game of constant innovation!

But what sort of game was it? What was this Frankenstein he was creating? As the wind howled around him, Garfield knew it was something never done before. It was, according to his taxonomy, a new essence. It wasn't just a card game. It was a trading-card game. With its unique combination of luck and skill, it would reward intelligence, intuition and cunning, strategy and creativity. For a new generation of mental athletes, it would be a beacon.

3. THE MAGIC BULLET

"Jon is slow and fat! Jon is slow and fat! Jon is slow and fat!"

As the chant closed in, Finkel backed against the cold metal locker in a bare concrete room that smelled like waxy lime deodorant and musty nylon gym bags. Surrounding him were the old familiar twisted faces, the bullies of New Jersey. It was a nightmare. Same jerks. Same hell. Same as it ever was. The pale angular mottled boys around him chanting "Jon is slow and fat!"

But this wasn't a bad dream. Stinkel was back.

After three years safely ensconced in England, seventeen-year-old Finkel returned to New Jersey in 1995 when his dad took a job back in the States. Now here he was, doomed again. Even worse, the instigator of the chant was a scrawny loudmouth twerp who was even lower on the Nerd Pyramid than Finkel. The twerp was the worst kind of nerd, Finkel stewed, an outcast geek who acted like a cocky brainiac even though he was hopelessly dumb. He bullied Finkel with the hopes of pulling himself one brick higher. But as he and the jerks quickly learned, Finkel wasn't the same old Stinkel anymore.

In a blur of blubber, Finkel leapt for the twerp, pulling him to the ground. The mottled boys hollered as Nerd One and Nerd Two rolled on the concrete floor. Finkel had the twerp by the ears, and he was pulling the kid's face higher and closer to his, like he was going to sink his teeth into the Fruit Roll-Up face and devour it whole. The jerks chanted. The twerp whimpered. Finkel eyed the kid's sad pathetic face, and let him go.

Finkel wasn't as slow and fat as he seemed. During his time in England, his bones had stretched into a six-foot-three frame, and his shoulders had filled out. And something else about him had changed. Even his parents took notice. Though their boy was growing even more overweight, and neglecting his tangled mop of hair, they didn't worry about him so much anymore. They took the hair as a sign of self-expression, and the body as a work-in-progress. Most important, Jon wasn't faking sick or moping around. "He's not acting like a victim anymore," Mark observed to Claire.

Their boy had tapped a new power: Magic.

Like a fellowship of nerds before him, Finkel had long escaped into fantasy worlds. The journey began with Tolkien novels. Before long, he graduated to fantasy games like Dungeons and Dragons. This led to live-action role-playing games—real-life spins of D&D in which he dressed up as a wizard and fought with costumed monsters in the caves near his home in England. In each experience, he molted from the weird fat kid into a hero. But nothing made him feel as heroic as Magic.

The moment he stumbled into the Fun and Games shop in England, and saw the guys wielding weird cards illustrated with swamp beasts and heaving ogres, Finkel was transfixed. Magic: The Gathering spoke to him on a subatomic level. Just when he was bottoming out, it revealed a glimpse of an identity. He wasn't a big lumbering geek anymore. In this game, as the owner of the shop explained as he shuffled the cards, "you're a wizard."

In Magic, he said, players are wizards dueling to the death. The object is to reduce the other's life score from 20 points to 0. Each player starts with his own deck. After shuffling, the players draw seven cards from the tops of their decks. There are two basic types of Magic cards: spells and lands. Spells are used to attack or defend against an opponent. Lands are the resources or money, essentially, one must pay to put spells into play. The bigger the spell, the more land cards a player must first lay down in order to use it.

The biker peeled off five cards and laid them face up on the table. There are five colors of Magic spells, he explained, red, black, white, blue, or green; each invokes its own flavor and personality. When drawing a red card, the player conjures the most fierce and ferocious creatures and enchantments—fire-breathing dragons, hellacious goblins. Green cards are spells and monsters of the earth—man-eating worms and thorn-covered spirits. Black cards invoke death and disease, monsters from black lagoons and tarlike poisons. Blue draws the magic of the sea and sky; white conjures lawful clerics and angels.

Each card bears a fantastical illustration of the magic form. A Howling Mine shows dark eyes lurking in a stone cave. There are White Castles, Blue Clones, Desert Twisters, Dingus Eggs, Dwarven Warriors, monsters drooling and bleeding and towering and growling, writhing in swamps and bursting into flames. They look like comic book covers or Wacky Pack fantasy cards ripped from the pages of *Lord of the Rings*.

Underneath each illustration is text that explains the card's power. The biker peeled off a Howling Mine, which read "Each player draws one extra card during his or her draw phase." Some spells immobilize players for a set number of turns, some let you draw cards from their stack. Others inflict damage. Two numbers in the lower-right corner of the card illustrate a card's power (how many points it takes from an opponent when played) and toughness (the strength of its defense). Depending on how the cards are used for attack or defense, the players' scores rise and fall accordingly.

As Finkel listened, he could see the similarities to bridge or chess—the strategy, the give-and-take of offensive and defensive plays. But as the biker noted, it's like a chess game in which every player assembles his own unique army of pieces. To play, each person needs his own deck of sixty, but the cards can be selected from thousands available at stores. Players pick and choose the cards with which they compete; the decks are built—or constructed—prior to the start of the game.

That meant Finkel could go out and buy or trade Magic cards, rifle through the spells he liked, and put them into a stack. Maybe a few Drudge Skeletons, an Energy Flux. Maybe Black Fear and Red Fireballs and Flying Carpets. It's like brewing up a chemistry kit, stocking a bat belt with gadgets. The decks are as unique and varied as their players. They reveal their creator's personality. A red deck is ferocious. A blue one is controlling. Finkel forked over his cash, and pedaled home with his first pack of Magic cards to discover what his color might be.

Before long, he was swimming in silvery Magic wrappers. At home, he'd stay up all hours ripping open packs of cards and selecting, or "drafting," which ones to use. As with creating a good recipe, he wanted to have all the right ingredients, the right balance of powers to unleash. At school, while his teacher droned on about trigonometry, he'd scribble his ultimate list of Magic cards in his notebook.

Finkel became obsessed. The kid who had been the fastest to learn his Torah portion for his bar mitzvah, the quickest at the quiz bowl, found the challenge of his life. Overnight, the game accomplished what no teacher or class had done: it turned him on. When he was constructing his decks, he felt creative, strategic. When he sat down to play, he became completely engaged, intuiting when to cast spells and how to pace the game. He had to both think ahead, anticipating moves and plays, and be in the moment, reading and responding to his opponent's actions.

While in England, Finkel spent every night at Fun and Games, honing his game, racking up his wins. This was an entirely new arena, a different way to compete. Just because he was a nerd didn't mean he didn't want to compete. It unleashed his power. He could use it to wrestle a loudmouth twerp to the ground in the locker room and cast his spell on the bad boys of Fanwood once and for all.

Tap Fierce Finkel. Target Jersey Dicks. Damage 10.

And don't call him Stinkel again.

"New Jersey Transit to Trenton! Track Six! All aboard!"

It was ten in the morning as the loudspeaker crackled throughout Pennsylvania Station, the train depot in New York City. Coffee burned. Doughnut glaze congealed. Bodies shifted fitfully on benches under mounds of plastic bags and newspapers. As the announcer's voice screeched again, one person rose gruffly from a bench: a large boy with matted curls and a Fruit Roll-Up falling off his chest. Finkel blearily checked his watch, and yawned. It was time to start playing Magic again.

He had been up all night again at the Neutral Ground, a game shop nearby on Twenty-sixth Street. Rather than schlepping home to Jersey, only to come back the next day, he devised a more efficient solution: sleeping in Penn Station, then returning to the shop when it opened in the morning. Now that he had found a calling playing cards, he would do anything to become the best.

Neutral Ground occupied the fourth floor of a building that also housed a modeling agency. Finkel and other misshapen gamers would cram into the rickety elevator with gazellelike blondes. When the doors opened on a hallway plastered with dragon posters, they knew whose floor they had arrived at. Neutral Ground's large loft space had exposed pipes and scuffed wooden floors. The front of the shop bulged with rows of geek gear: Magic cards, model gnomes, giant stuffed tetrahedral dice. Behind the counter, a dozen long card tables teemed with players. It resembled what one would imagine seeing at an underground poker club, but for kids. Instead of beers and cigarettes, the tables were covered with Mountain Dews and potato chips.

Since the 1970s, shops like this one—and Fun and Games, the store Finkel frequented back in England—had become community centers for players of D&D. After Magic was introduced in 1993, the shops initially embraced it as another role-playing game. With its ghoulish pictures of monsters and spells, after all, it certainly looked the part. But as the gamers quickly learned, Magic was a Trojan ogre; it carried something quite different inside. With its head-to-head competition, fast play, and strategic action, the game wasn't about touchy-feely things like building one's character, working as a team, and going on quests. The object was to whittle down an opponent's score from 20 to 0. It was about destruction and victory. It was a sport.

With his stomach hanging over his baggy jeans and his unruly Jewfro, Finkel became a fixture at the Ground, as it was commonly called. With his sharp skills and ruthless plays, he was tough to ignore or, for that matter, like. Just as when he had loudly ridiculed kids at his elementary school when they wrote down the wrong answers, Finkel didn't hesitate to correct Magic players when they made poor moves. He'd belittle them, scoff, and even reach over to grab and shuffle their cards to make sure they weren't cheating.

The arrogant behavior caught the attention of the two top players at Neutral Ground: brothers Steve and Dan O'Mahoney-Schwartz. Like Finkel, the OMS brothers, as they were known, were teenagers big in brain and body. Even heavier than Finkel, they grew up as street-savvy kids in Brooklyn, the sons of a teacher and a financial analyst, attending all the best magnet schools. Also like Finkel, they knew they were smarter than their teachers, and wouldn't hesitate to correct the adults when they were wrong, which was often.

Bored by high school, the OMS brothers began skipping classes to play Magic at Neutral Ground, where they quickly emerged as the guys to beat. When Finkel, this cocky kid from New Jersey (their rival state no less!) slaughtered them readily on their home turf, they hit the roof. Then they invited him out for burritos at Taco Bell.

Cut from such a similar mold, Finkel and the OMS brothers became instant buddies. On weekends, Finkel would take the train to their house in Sheepshead Bay, eating their mom's home cooking while poring over the latest Magic cards. After long nights gaming at Neutral Ground, Finkel and the OMS brothers would deconstruct their games over mounds of Burrito Supremes. They'd discuss Counterspells cards over cheeseburgers, Dragon Engines over Dairy Queen Blizzards, Sleight of Minds over Big Gulps.

Magic players began to derisively call Steve OMS and Finkel, now inseparable, Chubby and 'Fro. Finkel jokingly nicknamed the trio the Obesum Threesome. But mostly he just called them his friends.

Finkel wasn't the only misfit kid finding himself—and a community—through this game of cards. Magic had grown into a full-fledged cultural phenomenon. The success started with Wizards' shrewd sense of viral, grassroots marketing. Rather than distributing Magic to major chains like Toys 'R' Us or Wal-Mart, they circulated it to small hobby shops and conventions where, they felt, gamers could not only buy their product, but have a supportive environment within which to learn and play.

In the summer of 1993, Wizards' cherubic thirty-two-year-old founder Peter Adkinson and his new wife packed a van with Magic cards and drove down the West Coast to demonstrate the product at stores. During their first few stops at shops similar to Gandalf's Den and Neutral Ground, they were greeted by small, disinterested groups of geeks who didn't know what to make of these cards. Magic certainly looked like a fantasy game, but as Adkinson gleefully showed, it sure didn't play like one. What sort of heretical game was this anyway?

As the Adkinsons' road trip progressed, word of Magic spread among the tight-knit gamer community, online and off. With each stop, the Adkinsons found themselves greeted by larger and larger crowds. By the time the couple pulled up to the last shop on their trip, they were met with video cameras—and a red carpet. Peter phoned Garfield urgently. Something, he said, was on.

It didn't let up. The next month in Milwaukee, Wisconsin, Wizards stormed GenCon, the convention, founded by the creators of Dungeons and Dragons, that had long been ruled by fantasy role-playing games. Though Magic had originally been conceived by Adkinson as a time-killer between rounds of D&D, the conventioneers playing the game in the halls and stairwells proved the cards were plenty compelling on their own. Wizards stole the show, and sold out its stock. Upstairs in their suite, Garfield and the others from the company dumped the $25,000 cash on the bed and, in a Hollywood moment, threw the bills up in the air saying "We're rich! We're rich!"

They got richer. The first printing of 10 million Magic cards was expected to last an entire year. It lasted only six weeks. More than 300 million Magic cards were sold instead. Brought to shelves for $100,000—essentially the cost of printing and packaging—the game made $2 million in its first six months, and $57 million in its second year. By 1995 the game was pulling in $127 million a year, with a half billion cards in circulation. Magic fever had gripped the world. Newspapers said it was destined to join the ranks of perennials like Monopoly, Risk, and Scrabble. As *People* magazine gushed, it marked the dawn of "Generation Hex."

Like many other youth phenomena, however, Magic stirred up—and benefited from—its share of controversy. Kids fought over it; in Madison, Wisconsin, news spread of a Magic mugging in which a player leaving a game shop was clubbed over the head for his cards. As a result, schools banned it. Parents blamed it for suicides and decried it as evil. "The Devil has moved to Bedford, bag and baggage, and he is settling in," the grandmother of an elementary school player in Bedford, New York, told the *New York Times*. "These cards are everywhere, and the language on them is taken straight from Satan. These children are exhorted to cast spells on each other. I don't even call this a game."

But Wizards of the Coast, which thirty-one-year-old Garfield now co-owned, called it a gold mine. Garfield had spent a couple of years teaching and completing his Ph.D., but he soon devoted himself to games full-time. For an underdog who once never dared dream of making games for a living, he was suddenly sitting atop one of the biggest companies in the industry. His breakthrough design (which he patented) for a trading card game, it turned out, also made for a breakthrough business model.

Because Magic players could build decks from a pool of cards, Wizards was in the unique position of printing up new batches of cards throughout the year. The starter set of sixty cards and a forty-four-page rule book cost about $8. To stay on top of the game, Magic fans would have to pedal to their neighborhood stores to buy the latest new cards, which were sold in $3 blister packs. Magic had become the baseball cards of a new generation.

The retail world had a term for such a self-sustaining business model: repeat purchase. Gamers called it Magic crack. And *Brandweek* magazine dubbed Wizards, Marketers of the Year. Wizards couldn't print the stuff fast enough. In Sacramento, California, thieves broke into a game shop at night and swiped a box of newly released blister packs—but left full payment in cash on the register. They didn't want to steal the cards, they just couldn't wait until morning.

There was, however, a hitch to Wizards' master plan—and a potentially crippling one. Magic, like any new game or toy, had to fight against the industry's biggest demon: living and dying as a fad. Garfield had always wanted to create something classic, like poker. The market seemed to have other ideas.

When a player ripped open a new set of Magic cards, he received forty-four common cards chosen randomly, fourteen uncommon cards, and two rare cards. The rarer the card, the more powerful it is in play. For example, one of the rarest—and most coveted—is a spell card called Black Lotus. When tapped, it instantly adds 3 so-called mana of any single color to a player's well, which meant he could quickly and surprisingly unleash some wicked attacks.

Sensing an underground business, speculators began buying up the rarer Magic cards and turning them over at a premium. On the road, they'd pawn Magic cards for money, paying their way for hotels and meals. In Japan, the Magic craze was in full swing and the cards were more valuable than ever. American players would travel with suitcases full of cards, trading them with newbie collectors, then pawning them in foreign countries. On a good weekend, a Magic dealer could hustle an extra $5,000—as much as their friends could make in a year dunking fries at McDonald's. Rumors began circulating that Magic cards were so valuable that drug dealers were using them to launder cash. Considering the game's global popularity, it was just outrageous enough to be true.

With speculators jacking up card values, the ordinary players would soon be priced out of the market and the business would crash. If Magic was going to survive, it had to shift from being cards that people collected to a game that people played. A friend of Garfield's from Penn named George "Skaff" Elias, now brand manager for Magic, had the answer: make Magic a sport for real.

Though the game had been initially introduced to the fantasy gaming market, it hadn't taken long for it to bare its competitive teeth. The game had more in common with poker than D&D. So why not market the game in this fashion and, even better, throw in some powerful seed: cash.

The idea of playing cards for money, of course, was nothing new. And Garfield, the erudite gamer, understood the power of the money game. He had long been an avid poker player; in graduate school, he even sold shares of himself under the rubric of Royal Flush Enterprises. Though Royal Flush proved to be just that, the presence of money, he observed, added an entirely different dimension to a game. It gave players a way to keep score. And with something less ephemeral than emotions or trophies at stake, it instantly made the action more interesting. That's why people love poker, Garfield thought. They were vested in it beyond just the desire to win. They wanted their opponent to reach into his pocket and hand over hard-earned cash.

Garfield had originally designed Magic to utilize an ante. The idea was that, before a round of play, competitors would each offer up a card instead of a chip. The winner took the loser's card home. In practice, however, gamers proved too finicky to give their cards away, and the Magic ante died. But by putting some high-priced prizes on the table at organized tournaments, maybe Wizards could bring that fire back.

By 1995, Magic tournaments were being held around the world under an NFL-style outfit called the Duelist Convocation International, or DCI. But the DCI event was relatively small stuff, like a Street Fighter II tournament at the neighborhood minimall. Wizards needed to step up the game. As they began researching sports marketing, they discovered two approaches to cash prizes: spread the wealth to a wide number of players, hoping that the cash stimulates interest at the grassroots level, or take a more ambitious—and riskier—gamble by throwing the bulk of the cash at only the players on top.

The latter model applied to any big sport on the planet: basketball, football, tennis; the best players became professionals, and got gobs of money. Once elevated to star status, a Michael Jordan became the role model for aspiring basketball players in neighborhoods around the world. Sports marketers called this the "aspirational model." Wizards wanted in.

Garfield and company decided to create a so-called Pro Tour, open to only the best players, culled from qualifying tournaments around the world. The victory kids would appear on the cover of Magic's answer to *Sports Illustrated,* a magazine later called *Sideboard.* If the plan worked, the payoff would be tremendous—inspiring wannabe pros at game shops around the world, and elevating Magic into a new kind of sport for a new generation of disenfranchised brainiacs. It could create, as Garfield put it, "mental athletes." But the prospect of launching a new brain sport was predicated on one thing: finding the Michael Jordan of Magic.

Wizards hit the phones with the news: the first Pro Tour of Magic was coming to New York, February 1996, be there. They called game shops around the country, because their star could be anywhere. Maybe he was in San Francisco, competing in the back of a noodle shop. Maybe he was in Tampa, slumped over the wheel of his truck, buried in Magic cards after smashing through a game shop's plate-glass window. Or maybe he was in New York City, sleeping on a bench in Penn Station and dreaming of cards.

The Obesum Threesome stomped up from the subway at Broadway and Lafayette in New York City, headfirst into a blizzard. It was February 17, 1996, outside the Puck Building, a one-hundred-year-old redbrick Romanesque building on the edge of Soho and the Village. The time for the first Magic Pro Tour competition had come. And Finkel was ready to play.

After hearing the kids at the Ground discuss the Pro Tour, Finkel burned to compete. But the event was invite only. And who was going to invite a total unknown? Rather than sit by the side, he picked up the phone and called Wizards. "My name is Jon Finkel," he loudly declared, "and I was wondering if I could come to the Pro Tour." What the hell, the staff at Wizards thought, if the kid had the balls to call up and ask for an invitation, how could they say no?

Careful not to slide on the ice, Finkel and the OMS brothers lumbered inside. Standing by the door was Garfield in an Aztec-patterned vest and mismatched socks, looking out the window. How cool, Finkel thought, recognizing Magic's creator, there's the mad scientist himself in person, the one responsible for all of this. "Okay," Garfield sighed, "whose bright idea was it to have the first Pro Tour in New York in the middle of winter?"

But despite the bad weather, as Finkel could see, the Magic players had come to the inaugural Pro Tour in full force. Three hundred forty-seven of the best players in the world showed up to compete all weekend for a total of $60,000 in prize money. Finkel found hordes of them swarming the regal ballroom, a large space with glossy wooden floors and white columns wrapped in pearly strings of lights. Others crowded the antique bar, an area reserved for the Masters—the 239 players over the age of eighteen. The night before had been an open bar for the legal-age Masters, and, by the look of their bloodshot eyes, it seemed that some were still recovering.

Though this was the first Pro Tour event, an elite group of players had already emerged from small-scale tournaments held at game shops around the country. Twenty-seven-year-old Shawn "Hammer" Regnier, a game shop owner, swaggered around with his Popeye arms bulging from his sleeveless blue shirt. He wore dark sunglasses and a black bandanna bearing his nickname. Before discovering Magic, Hammer got his moniker as a professional arm wrestler, where he was known for trash-talking opponents into submission. When requested, he'd obligingly arm wrestle a Magic geek, waiting until the final second before slamming the kid's bony arm to the table. At one Magic tournament, a player got so scared at the prospect of competing against Hammer that he spent the match in the bathroom throwing up.

Near Hammer stood Mark Justice, the Luke Skywalker of the game. Blond, blue-eyed, clean-cut in a beige suit, Justice was a twenty-six-year-old Mormon from West Valley City, Utah. Like Hammer, he, too, ran his own game shop. Feared for his steady, machinelike play, Justice had won a big Magic event to become the U.S. National Champion the year before. Everyone considered him the best in the world—a fine contender to become the sport's first superstar.

Before the event began, Garfield stepped tentatively in front of a microphone to address the crowd. "I've taken games seriously for a long time," he said. "The reason I take games seriously is because I consider them the intellectual counterpart to sports. I think they exercise your brain. I would love to see games raised to the stature of intellectual sports. Thanks, and have fun."

Finkel enthusiastically joined the applause, and felt electrified by his first brush with this new world. Serious referees in black buttonup Magic shirts dispersed across the room. Players closed in on the tables. Tension filled the air. It seemed just like a real sport—except for the guy dressed up like a giant minotaur in a furry brown suit with two big black horns coming out of his head, who wandered through the crowd.

Despite the pleas of Skaff, the guy who dreamed up the Pro Tour at Wizards, the marketing team insisted that the minotaur be at the event. They weren't buying the whole Magic-as-sport plan yet. As far as they were concerned, this was still a fantasy game and the minotaur was there to drive home that point. Skaff, who had talked a big sports marketer from a company called ProServe into coming to observe the event, felt humiliated. He vowed to send the minotaur packing.

Finkel took his seat in the ballroom upstairs, where 108 Magic players under age eighteen competed in the Juniors event for a $12,000 scholarship. Outside the windows, he could see the blizzard enveloping Soho. After years of being beaten down and pissed upon, he was finally stepping up to the plate. For weeks, he had meticulously assembled his most potent deck of spells and creatures. It was a deeply scientific process, analyzing the cards for their traits and handpicking each one like a wizard preparing for battle.

It took only minutes for Finkel to see how potent a wizard he had become. He destroyed his first opponent, whittling the kid's life down from 20 to 0 in a flash, until he erupted from the table with a triumphant smack of his paws. "Yes!" Finkel loudly declared in his New Jersey accent. Steve OMS gave him a high five.

When Finkel sat down for his next round, however, a Wizards referee pulled him aside. "Your opponent says you used an illegal deck," the ref explained.

"What?" Finkel said. "I didn't cheat."

The referee held up three cards. Finkel had lost the cards in an earlier round, and apparently forgot to shuffle them back into his deck. According to Magic rules, it was like a football team playing with only nine players on the field; it didn't necessarily put them at an advantage, but it was an infraction all the same. "You won that game illegally," the ref concluded. "We're going to have to give you a game loss."

Finkel exploded. "That is bullshit!" he screamed awkwardly. The OMS brothers tried to calm him down. Maybe he did forget to shuffle the cards, maybe it was an infraction. But it was so unjust. He couldn't take this lying down. "I want to talk to a higher-up!" he announced. Magic players began looking over at the awkward fat kid flapping his arms. Hearing the commotion, Skaff, a tall guy with large crooked glasses and a goatee, made his way over. Finkel was wheezing, red-faced. "I want my fifty-dollar entry back!" he cried.

What's wrong with this kid? Skaff thought. The last thing he needed was a scene at Magic's first big outing. "Look," Skaff said, quietly, "I'm sure you're a smart guy. You can probably win. But you have to understand that we have these rules to protect you."

"I know!" Finkel cried, even more loudly. "But I didn't cheat!" He didn't leave the cards out intentionally. He didn't break the rules. The cards, which were worthless, must have just fallen out of his deck. He had won that match by his brains and preparation, and for what? To have it all taken away. The injustice stirred up all his old feelings of meaninglessness and persecution. The smart nice kid was going to finish last again. The rage filled his chest and arms and face and he burst out sobbing, just like that time in the gym at school, hot tears skiing down his face.

Skaff quickly pulled the blubbering kid aside. "Hey, come on," he said, heading for a corner. "Look, you tell me you're honest, I believe you're honest. But if someone at the table next to you is playing with fifty-nine cards, you'd want me to give them a game loss because they might be cheating, right?"

Finkel sniffled. "I might as well just withdraw from the tournament," he whimpered.

Skaff looked at this poor kid. Finkel was no Hammer. It would have been easy to let him just walk away. But he was a Magic player nonetheless, one of the disenfranchised boys who, through this game, was beginning to find his way. Skaff wanted to stick by him.

"Look," Skaff said, "stay in the tournament. I promise you, you still have a chance. Stay in the tournament and you'll be okay."

Finkel wiped his nose on his sleeve. "Okay," he said, and went back to play.

By the end of the weekend, the tournament reached the finals. The regal Puck was littered with Magic wrappers and crushed soda cans. The minotaur sat in his chair and yawned. Downstairs in the Masters arena, a chunky twenty-six-year-old with a double chin and blue bandanna was heads-up against a hotheaded twenty-five-year-old from Pantin, France.

The Frenchman had something of a reputation behind him. At one event in Europe, he flew off the handle after what he thought was a bad call, and shoved a referee against the wall. Weary, eyes bloodshot, they dripped with sweat. Onlookers crowded the area for a view. Some even pulled tables out of the kitchen, and climbed on top to look over the heads. There was dead silence as the two finalists peeled the cards from their decks.

The marketing guy from ProServe pulled Skaff aside and whispered, "I don't know what the hell is going on," he said, "but there's drama here. This is a sport." The bandanna man won, to a burst of applause, taking home a check for $12,000. Skaff had proved that Magic was a sport. It was time to send the minotaur home once and for all.

As the crowd cleared, Skaff ran into Finkel coming out of the elevator. "Hey," Finkel yelped, "thanks for getting me to stay in the tournament!" He showed him a check for a $1,000 scholarship, and a smile that was even bigger. "Look what I won!"

Skaff watched the big curly-haired boy as he plodded giddily into the slush.

Black Lotus 0

Mono Artifact

Adds 3 mana of any single color of your choice to your mana pool, then is discarded. Tapping this artifact can be played as an interrupt.

Illus. © Christopher Rush

4. JERSEY KIDS VS. DEAD GUYS

There aren't a lot of options for the boys of Linden, New Jersey. Twenty-three miles west of New York City, it's a town of modest homes, lined up alongside one another, with neighbors in undershirts peering over their chain-link fences to tell each other to keep their dogs from barking all night.

Up in their bedrooms, the boys crank Bon Jovi on their headphones, and leaf through the sports section of the Newark *Star-Ledger,* catching up on the Giants and Nets. After school and on weekends, they grab basketballs from their closets and dribble down to the closest park, where others linger in backward baseball caps and baggy shorts. After night falls, they stand around with their shirts matted to their chests, smoking cigarettes, swapping sordid stories of Linden girls, and slugging each other in the arms.

In 1996, there was one other place for the other Linden boys to compete: the Outer Realms. In the early nineties, the Realms, as it was known, had been in a tiny storefront split down the middle— one side sold records, the other, Dungeons and Dragons parapher- nalia. Eventually the stacks of Bon Jovi CDs got squeezed out, and the Realms expanded into a new store across the street from Carvel Ice Cream. There was a bigger game in town, Magic: The Gathering. And the biggest player of all, literally and figuratively, was eighteen- year-old Jon Finkel.

Though he still ventured into New York to play with the OMS brothers at Neutral Ground, the Realms was closer to his new home: Rutgers, the state university of New Jersey. Despite scoring a near perfect 1550 (800 verbal, 750 math) on the SAT, Finkel lazily wrote his college essay by hand, and failed to get accepted to his dream school of Princeton. He knew he had disappointed his parents, who had hoped for an Ivy League education. Jenny, Jon's younger sister, was certainly on the "right" path, acing her classes and eyeing Co- lumbia University. But Mark and Claire Finkel had by now stopped expecting anything conventional from Jon. It was even harder to tell him what to do. They just hoped he'd graduate from college and not let distractions get in his way.

At Rutgers, Finkel did his best to fit in, talking sports with the guys in the dorm. But he still felt like an outsider. Finkel tried not to let the freshman blues get him down. He would just take the train to the Realms to blow off steam in Magic. But as the game became more of a sport, he found his share of hazing and competition there, too. It came in the form of his first rival, David Bachmann.

Two years younger than Finkel, Bachmann was a wiry, hyper brat from Linden who had ruled the Realms long before the big loud kid from Rutgers crashed his scene. The son of a trucking company CEO, Bachmann was a bright math student, who fought doggedly against being a geek. Bachmann, who played on his school's basket- ball and baseball teams, loved trash-talking, acting tough, and intim- idating other players. He had no interest in fantasy or *Lord of the*

Rings; when a friend showed him Magic: The Gathering, he didn't care about the "flavor"; he just saw another way to kick ass.

Before Finkel arrived, Bachmann was doing just that: traveling to the local Magic tournaments, and pocketing $10,000 by the time he was fifteen. The Realms was his home court, the place he practiced and refined his game. His best friend there was a charismatic player nicknamed Happy John. Scrappy and competitive, their reputation was that they would do anything and everything to win at Magic tournaments. People talked about how they berated their opponents. They gloated. And when their opponents weren't looking, they made sure all their best Magic cards got "shuffled" to the tops of their decks. They garnered their own nickname, the Jersey Kids. When Finkel showed up trying to whip them at their own game, on their own turf no less, they did what any other small-town athlete would do: they trashed him.

One day, Finkel had gone outside to get some ice cream at Carvel. He stood in front of the revolving trays of delectable treats: Tommy the Turkey cakes, Flying Saucers. Despite having latched on to the empowering focus of Magic, he was eating as much as ever. In England, he had developed an appetite for McDonald's Happy Meals. At home, he still disappeared into the bathroom after dinner to gorge on Fruit Roll-Ups. Now there was Carvel—creamy and dreamy like candy-colored Magic cards—red strawberry, blue blueberry, green mint, black licorice, white chocolate.

As Finkel waddled into the Realms with his ice cream, he found Happy John and Bachmann slapping down cards midgame. A small group of watching players nodded, impressed. Bachmann looked up at Finkel, the chubby kid who had recently dyed his hair an awkward shade of red. Hey look, Bachmann would tease, it's "Ronald McFinkel!"

Finkel squeezed into a seat, shrugging off the latest derisive nickname. After years of abuse, even from nerds like this kid, he had become callous enough to let it slide. It was a natural defense, a way of protecting himself. But now he also had another way to respond:

he reached into his pocket and pulled out his Magic deck. The deck was a meticulously crafted thing. He had spent hours at home, brewing up just the right combination of Lava Bursts and Hydro-blasts, just the right dose of Jester's Caps and Icy Manipulators. Sure enough, the brew proved potent enough to whip Bachmann into a pulp. In a flurry of cards, Finkel cut Bachmann's score from 20 to 0 and won again. Bachmann would make him pay.

After a trip to the bathroom, Finkel came back to scoop up his winning deck, but it was gone. He looked under the table, under his chair. From above, he could hear Bachmann snickering. Bachmann had been hiding his cards on a regular basis, and never seemed to tire of this and other practical jokes at Finkel's expense. One time he sold Finkel what was promised to be a real Black Lotus—one of the most valuable cards in the Magic deck. By the time he got home, Finkel could see the ink rubbing off on his hands; the Black Lotus was a fake.

But Finkel took the pranks in stride. After so many years on his own, he figured this was just how young guys treated each other. Even when he was crawling around the floor, he considered the Kids his friends.

As Magic exploded in popularity, Finkel and the Jersey Kids were far from alone. The Realms was but one of thousands of game shops around the world nurturing this new arena of competition. From Linden to London, New York to Norway, Brooklyn to Budapest, all the math and fantasy geeks who had had nowhere to compete before were swarming into these stores.

Each shop developed its own reputation, based on the skills of the players; your store became your identity. At local tournaments, the shops would vie against one another for cash and bragging rights. For often the first time in their lives, boys who were ordinar-ily last in the lineup for dodgeball had a shot at being the best. And there was nothing better than making the Magic Pro Tour.

Since the first Pro Tournament in New York, Wizards, with Richard Garfield's blessing, pumped millions of dollars into the action. The company developed a sophisticated competitive structure around the professional events. To participate in the four Pro Tour events around the world, players had to first qualify through a local tournament, or "meatgrinder." In addition, Wizards began holding smaller-scale "grand prix" events from Amsterdam to Rio de Janeiro. They struck a deal with ESPN2 to broadcast the events. They beefed up their monthly issues of *Sideboard,* their answer to *Sports Illustrated.*

The gamble to transform Magic from a fad to a sport had paid off. Just as in football or baseball, there was a new kind of aspirational model in place. Kids at game shops around the world aspired to rise to the professional level. Though some girls played, too, the overwhelming majority of players were boys under the age of twenty-five.

To compete, they had to stay on top of their game, which meant buying every new set of Magic cards and incorporating them into their play. Unlike, say, poker, Magic necessitated a new purchase every few months. Instead of spending $1.95 once in a lifetime for a deck of ordinary playing cards, millions of Magic sharks were spending $500 per year.

With its relatively cheap overhead and built-in repeat purchase model, Wizards became the envy of the hobby business. The company expanded its offices in Seattle to accommodate its 120 employees; Wizards had become Mecca for fantasy freaks and misfit gamers. At any moment, Garfield might wander down the halls in his bow tie to find two purple-haired kids in black capes pretending to be vampires. Garfield, once a misfit himself who dreamed of making games for a living, had divined not only an industry, but a culture and community as well. Cementing its mystique and reputation, Wizards purchased TSR, the fledgling company behind Dungeons and Dragons. For Garfield and his peers, lifelong players of D&D, the move was more than symbolic; Magic had stormed the castle.

The more successful Wizards became, the more they invested back into what they considered to be the source of their power, the Pro Tour scene. They wanted to take it to the ultimate level: increasing the purse so that, as in other sports, the best competitors could make a living at the game. And naturally, the more money they threw at the young cardplayers, the more like sharks the boys became.

To prepare for the events, players formed training teams—small collectives who pooled knowledge to increase their individual chances of winning on the road. At Magic tournaments, many of the events were based on so-called constructive play. This meant that, before the competition, players constructed or built their own sixty-card decks, culled from the hundreds of available cards in the Magic pool.

Given the millions of possible card combinations, building a deck was a science. Each card had its own power, and each power altered the game. So having just the right combination of Drudge Skeletons and Plague Rats was like mixing chemicals for the desired effect. And like the chemists they could easily have become, given their skills in math and science, the players formed almost academic research and development teams. As Mike Long, a Magic pro at James Madison University in Virginia, put it, the goal was to "articulate a harmonious functional scientific community."

Long, a prominent player on the scene, derived the idea from *Think and Grow Rich,* a pioneering self-help book by Napoleon Hill that had been commissioned by Andrew Carnegie. "When Carnegie and Thomas Edison and Henry Ford shared information," Long effused, "you could see a meteoric rise in their output. Their numbers blew up once they worked together! Let's bring that to Magic! It's the mastermind principle. Brains function like batteries. If you link them in series, you get a more powerful battery. But if you take one out of the series and flip it around, you get a meltdown. Let's build a better battery!" Long formed a group, Tongo Nation, and went to work.

He wasn't the only one. Out in California, Magic veteran Mark Justice formed a team called Pacific Coast Legends. In Pittsburgh, Pennsylvania, a group of students at Carnegie Mellon University formed Team CMU. In Ithaca, New York, a team of Cornell math students formed the Dead Guys, named after their favorite punk rock band. On any given night, someone could walk into a student lounge, Taco Bell, or dorm room and find a cluster of unshaven young men feverishly dealing Magic cards.

Once the players hit the road, however, it was every man for himself. Like poker in the Wild West, the early days on the Magic tournament scene became riddled with cheating, controversy, egos, and collusion. As one player put it, "Any game where you can manipulate your own deck, you can't prevent cheating."

Players marked cards, licking them so that the good ones stuck together, making them easy to find during a draw. They bent the corners, scratched signifiers on the backs. If the cards weren't marked, they could be controlled with a little sleight of hand. Players began "breaking the bridge" or "pile shuffling," a technique that assured that a prearranged stack of favorable cards remained at the top of the deck. As a precaution, the smart players began shuffling one another's decks before they'd sit down to play. But even such action didn't prevent controversy.

During one match, a powerful card called Cadaverous Bloom was found in Mike Long's lap; though he denied cheating, he received a disqualification. Rather than decrying the injustice, he milked his bad reputation to improve his gamesmanship. During a match, he'd climb up on his chair, squatting down on his feet as he arched over the table like a praying mantis, heckling his opponents while they played.

The players, many of whom were unschooled in competition, didn't know what to make of his behavior. Sometimes they'd simply cave in. Once, when Long was certain to lose, he showed the other player his hand and bragged, "You're done, let's go to the next game!" The player had no idea that the rest of Long's cards were complete garbage. But given Long's reputation, he buckled to the bluff—and conceded.

As reputations grew, big players like Long let the attention go to their heads. They had autograph hounds, nicknamed "barns" for barnacles, and even groupies, called ogresses. As the egos grew, so did the outrage. At a tournament in France, one player accused of cheating shocked the pencil-necked geeks by slugging a Wizards referee in the gut. During another event, Mark Justice, the fair-haired champ from Utah, leapt onto his chair and called for a player mutiny after Wizards disqualified one of his friends.

Like poker players, Magic pros raced for an edge wherever and whenever they could find it. Though there were certainly more honest players than dishonest ones, the hustlers and cheaters, not surprisingly, rode their waves of deception to the top of the sport. But there was one group of players who were prepared to do something about it: the Dead Guys.

Compared to the more straitlaced players on the scene, the Dead Guys, at first glance, looked like the criminal type. Their leader, Dave Price, had long dark hair, hoop earrings, and black painted fingernails, and favored punk rock T-shirts. Price was an aspiring poet, weaned on writers like Charles Bukowski and Jack Kerouac. He backpacked across Europe and drove by himself across America from one Magic event to another. Though he was studying computer science to please his parents, he had declared a second major in English literature, his real passion. What he liked most about his favorite writers, he said, was their "brutal honesty." On the Magic circuit, Price emulated brutal honesty in play.

At tournaments, Price and the Dead Guys began educating players on how to protect themselves against being hustled. They encouraged others to shuffle opponents' cards. On many occasions, sneaky players would "accidentally" tally a score wrong while they were playing; the Dead Guys urged everyone to keep track not only of their own scores, but of their opponent's, too.

Before long, some of the game's most esteemed champions began falling from grace. Even Justice, the so-called Stormin' Mormon, had descended into a shadow of his former self. At one event in Germany, he got caught up in a drinking challenge with some other players. By the end, he ran off for the bathroom. When Finkel inadvertently walked in on Justice, the former star looked up and slurred, "Don't let this happen to you."

Between the cheating and the controversies, Wizards suddenly began seeing their future stars go to waste. The Magic discussion groups raged with flames over how to deal with the unscrupulous sharks. "Cheaters should be publicly humiliated, shunned, disdained, and despised," posted one player. "They should not be looked at as exemplars of 'good' Magic players, they should be looked at as the lowest of the low—the shit that just happened to be blown in the door."

For the sport to reach the next level, Wizards desperately needed a new champion—someone both skilled and honest—to step up to the plate.

Late one night in New Brunswick, Finkel hunched over, deep in the glow of his computer, a bubbling soda in his paw, as he pored over the information on the screen. He wasn't studying biology or astronomy or class notes on economics; he was cramming Magic.

Like more and more players, Finkel had begun drawing power from the Internet. He could swap strategy in online chat groups, discuss psychology in forums, and play hands in multiplayer games. It was the perfect complement and conduit for the academic research being conducted by the teams of Magic players from Cornell to Carnegie Mellon. It put into practice a dictum that would benefit any cardplayer, from Magic to poker: share information, and prosper.

Finkel devoured the information like he consumed everything— voraciously. And, combined with his quick learning and fast analysis, he excelled. On the road, Finkel became known for mystifying even the top players with his uncanny reasoning skills. "Jon makes plays where you have no idea what he's doing," said a CMU player named Randy Buehler, "then three or four plays later, you get it, and realize how far he was thinking ahead."

Finkel became just as known for his tenacity. When faced with a losing hand, rather than give up, he would plow ahead—bluffing, maneuvering, and, ultimately, forcing his opponents to make a mistake. After one such embarrassing loss, a player who had the cards to prevail over Finkel folded out of sheer terror. "Jon Finkel decided to try to put an end to my streak," posted the player online. "He succeeded thanks to me being brain dead, when I conceded a game to him even though I wasn't dead."

While veteran Magic players descended into controversies of cheating and hustling, Finkel developed a reputation for his remarkable raw talent and unwavering composure. Long gone were the days when he would break down blubbering, as he did at his first Pro Tour event in New York. Now, even when he lost, which was less and less often, he remained sportsmanlike. When he won, there was no question in anyone's mind that, unlike the other Jersey Kids, he had earned it.

But outside of the game, Finkel's rising star came at a price. As 1997 progressed, he began showing up less and less frequently for classes, preferring to spend his time playing Magic online or pursuing his other new hobby, smoking pot. Unchallenged by his classes and bored at the prospect of a traditional nine-to-five job, he dreamed of a more independent future. By the end of his freshman year, the nineteen-year-old had flunked out of college. But he wasn't fazed. He had another plan.

"I really think I can make money playing Magic," he told his dad one night. "I feel like there's a good chance I'm the best player."

Mark Finkel squinted his eyes behind his glasses as if he was getting a migraine. Now that Jon had flunked out of school, he was back living at home. Meanwhile, his sister, Jenny, also a math prodigy, was pursuing a computer science degree at Columbia. What had happened to the gifted young boy?

Maybe, his dad thought, the family life was taking a toll. Now that Jon and Jenny were away at school, Mark and Claire had told the kids they were getting divorced. For Jon it came as no surprise; he never thought they seemed very happy together. But even such personal problems were no excuse for flunking out and becoming a teenage card shark, said his dad. "If you want to stay here without paying rent," Mark exploded, "then you better go out and get a real job!"

Finkel grudgingly obliged, getting a gig delivering pizzas at the local Domino's. Every time he slipped into his goofy uniform, he promised to prove his dad wrong—to show him that he could play cards for a living. Poker players did it, after all. Now, with Magic, a new generation of sharks could get their game on, too. Finkel had already begun to prove his point, taking home a $10,000 third-place prize at a Magic Pro Tour in Chicago in October 1997. With the Pro Tour making a stop in New York City in August 1998, he determined to rest his case by taking home a first-place win once and for all.

Finkel, wearing baggy khaki pants and a white Neutral Ground T-shirt, showed up at the New York event with his ever-present buddy Steve OMS by his side. But he had a new pal, too: David Williams. Half-black and half-Iranian, Williams was a handsome seventeen-year-old with short curls and a quietly burning intensity. Finkel had met Williams in Los Angeles, at a recent Pro Tour event, and though the two had dramatically different backgrounds, they clicked all the same.

Like Finkel, Williams used his exceptional brains to lift him out of a challenging childhood. His father, an Iranian, left his mother, Shirley, before David was born. To support herself and her son, Shirley worked as a stewardess for Delta Airlines and would be gone for days at a time while Williams stayed with his grandparents. When she returned, the two would catch up on lost time by playing Nintendo late into the night. Though extremely close with his mom, Williams would occasionally tell her that he wished he had a dad. Then she'd be gone again. Before long, Williams hardened to the point of not mentioning his father at all.

At school, Williams became obsessed with proving himself. But there was one problem: like Finkel, he was bad at sports. So, instead, he competed with his mind. If he scored a 99 on a test, he'd quickly check the room to see if anyone got 100. After breezing through his classwork at home, he'd head for the neighborhood Putt-Putt to battle kids at Street Fighter II. When he discovered Magic: The Gathering, he seized the power, even though he couldn't identify with the nerdy players it attracted. "You could assert your dominance on people who are less intelligent than you," Williams said. "You get to beat them at a game and prove you're smarter. I just beat you, so I'm better than you."

After being transferred to an accelerated magnet school, he spent every spare moment playing Magic. On the game shop courts, Williams became the guy to beat in town. But it didn't take long for him to hear about the up-and-coming kid on the Pro Tour circuit: Jon Finkel. With free flights that came with his mom's job, Williams hit the road to observe the rising star in action.

On the surface, the two couldn't have been more different. Though two years younger, Williams was a cool and confident ladies' man who considered Finkel the ultimate nerd. He thought Dungeons and Dragons was embarrassingly dorky, and had never read a fantasy book in his life. But Williams recognized something familiar in the big awkward kid. They shared a raw talent and intuitive sense of play; plus, they were among the brightest bulbs in an already luminescent crowd. They also knew how to crack each other up. After Williams's dismal performance early at a Pro Tour event, it became clear that the two had something to offer each other. Finkel was socially inept but a seasoned Magic pro; Williams was socially adept but unseasoned on the road. Though the bond was unspoken, they took each other on. Together, there was no telling how far they'd go.

But as Finkel and Williams arrived at the New York event, they were in for a fight. Top players from around the country swarmed underneath the towering ceiling of the Twenty-third Street Armory where the event was being held. Cards blanketed tables and floors, alongside silvery wrappers and pizza-stained paper plates. Refs, who had taken to wearing NFL-style black-and-white-striped shirts, roamed the hall. With crowds growing at these events and ESPN2 on hand to document the action, Wizards now splurged for giant simulcast screens to make sure no one missed a shuffle. The purse was good—$25,000 going to this weekend's winner alone. Players paced the halls. One had taken to licking the ear of another player for good luck.

By the time the quarterfinals arrived, three of the final eight competitors were Jersey Kids, including the notorious duo, Bachmann and Happy John. And the two were going to do anything, and everything, to make sure the number one seed, Finkel, wouldn't be the one taking home the prize.

Before the draft, the Jersey Kids were already swarmed with controversy. In a match for the second seed in the top eight, Happy John was allegedly observed "breaking the bridge," shuffling his cards for advantage, against his competitor. Though unsubstantiated, the incident chipped away at the happy-go-lucky reputation that he had enjoyed. Steve OMS even said to Finkel that he thought Happy John had conspired against him.

But Finkel refused to believe it. He still considered the Jersey Kids his friends. Despite all the pranks and insults at the Realms, Finkel had never once doubted that they were, deep down, on his side. He had grown accustomed to abuse. In fact, it was his ability to let things slide, to laugh off the mean jokes, that made him the cardplayer he was that day.

One key to being successful at cards, he knew, is consistency, to avoid losing one's cool and going "on tilt," as the poker players put it. That's what distinguishes the champions at the end of the day more than memorizing every strategy, reading every book, or watching every play. It's the mind game, the meta-game, the life game. Two players who know all the right moves will eventually get dealt all the same cards. The winner is the one who makes the fewest mistakes. Players are less prone to mistakes when they stay off tilt, when they remain cool. For Finkel, it was the great irony of feeling like a lifelong loser. The bullies beat the poker face into him.

As the Magic referees at the tourney explained, this was going to be a so-called booster draft, in which players, before competing, drafted their decks on the fly. Unlike the constructed decks, which were meticulously engineered prior to an event, booster drafts required intuition, gut play, and gamesmanship. After unsealing decks, players would go around the table taking turns selecting or "drafting" cards to use.

Some cards were chosen because they were capable of reducing an opponent's score by a larger number of points. Players also drafted according to their own personal strengths, weaknesses, and reads on what sort of decks their opponents were building. But as Finkel quickly observed, it seemed that Bachmann and Happy John, his supposed "team," had a few tricks up their sleeves.

Like any good poker player, he had been developing an intuitive ability to read tells—the subtle, nonverbal cues expressed by other players. As Finkel pored over his card choices, he noticed an almost telepathic exchange between Bachmann and Happy John. Players were not allowed to talk during drafts, to prevent collusion, but Finkel thought the two were in cahoots nonetheless. Before the draft, he surmised, they had preordained which types of cards they would each select, ensuring that they stood better chances of beating their opponents, including Finkel. There was no doubt about it, he realized; they were ganging up against him.

"Hey," Finkel said, approaching the two after the draft, "what the hell was that all about? You guys cheated me!" Bachmann and Happy John shrugged him off and went to play their opponents. There was still plenty of time left in the event, Finkel knew, and he hoped he'd get a chance to face off against the Jersey Kids before the end.

Making his way over to his assigned table, Finkel noticed a crowd looming nearby. Skinny kids in T-shirts and baseball caps hovered at the rail to watch Finkel, the number one seed, play. When he caught their glances, he felt electrified. After all these years on the bottom of the heap, he was on the verge of becoming a champion. All those qualities that had isolated him in the past—his smarts, his misfit fortitude—had finally found their place. And now, once and for all, he was going to show the world who Stinkel had become. He even reached out to his mom, calling her up and asking her to come into the city to watch him make good. She didn't hesitate, telling him she was on her way.

Finkel waved to the crowd as his quarterfinal match was about to begin. He reached across the table to shake his opponent's hand. But when he sat down to play, he just kept falling, crashing onto the floor and jamming his fingers into his hand. He let out a hapless scream, grabbing his paw, as the laughs erupted around him. Someone had pulled out his chair from under him. He scanned around, and found the red laughing face of Bachmann.

"Judge, judge!" Finkel cried. "Did you see that?" But no penalty came. Bachmann just mockingly jutted out his lower lip, and gloated. As the laughter subsided, Finkel lumbered up to Bachmann, and looked down on the boy. "Fuck you," he wheezed. "I owe you one."

He soon got his chance to deliver. After both won their quarter-final matches, Finkel and Bachmann were paired in the semis. It was the main event in more ways than one. Word of the chair-pulling incident had made it throughout the players. David Williams, who knew the Kids, was disgusted by the behavior; Finkel deserved respect, not abuse.

But Bachmann couldn't care less. He even rhapsodized about it online, posting that making Finkel cry "only brings a smile to my face, because he's 6 foot 5 and is a disgrace. I told him once, and I told him twice, that no matter what I will never be nice . . . I don't really care what other people think, because public enemy #1 is the fink." The match with Finkel, Bachmann wrote, was "the match of my life, against the kid who will never have a wife." Now, as the crowd closed in, everyone wanted to see if Finkel would avenge himself.

Finkel and Bachmann silently marched behind the judges to the special back room where the final Top 8 matches were being filmed by ESPN2 and broadcast on the giant screen outside. Finkel's mom, Claire, arrived to find her son's face flashing across the monitors, with a crowd of players cheering him on. Although she knew of his Magic success, she'd never seen anything like this—the cameras, the action, and the fans, all there for her boy. And she hardly expected the treatment she'd get when she mentioned to the crowd that she was Finkel's mom.

"Finkel's mom?" gushed one of his fans. "It's Finkel's mother!" he announced to his friends, who quickly made room in the seats. "Please," the fan said, "come sit over here. It'd be an honor!"

Claire smiled appreciatively and took a seat. After years of seeing her boy ignored by his peers, it was heartening to find him the center of attention. Though she and Mark were still reeling from Finkel's poor showing at Rutgers, she was trying to put more faith in her boy. She knew he was smart, smarter, she felt, than she was herself. She gambled that he would find his way. And now, under the bright lamps, she was seeing him in a new light. Maybe this Magic game had more to it than she thought.

As the cameras closed in, Finkel and Bachmann sat in their chairs and began playing for the best out of five games. But Finkel quickly fell behind. By the beginning of the fourth game, he was down 2 to 1. The crowd was stunned. By now, they were all on Finkel's side. Even the Dead Guys, the scrappy heroes of the scene who had been shut out of the Top 8, stuck around to see if the kid could dust the punk. It was a crossroads moment not just for Finkel but for this emerging sport. Would the future of Magic be ruled by degenerate brats or a worthy new star?

In a flurry of beasts and spells, Finkel took the fourth game to tie it all up. The fifth would decide who would move on to the finals. It was a neck-and-neck battle until Finkel reached into his deck and pulled out a Grave Pact, a card illustrated with three ghastly, bloated minstrels serenading a corpse in a crypt. It bears a fitting quote on the bottom: "The bonds of loyalty can tie one to the grave." When tapped, it requires the other player to discard his powerful creatures every time you relinquish one of your own. But as Finkel put Grave Pact into play, he would bear these bonds of loyalty no more. He had successfully whittled Bachman's score down from 20 to 0, and won the game. Bachmann was dead.

Outside the small room, the crowd roared. Finkel rose from his chair and got besieged by fans. The Dead Guys raced over, patting him on the back. Finkel's mother hugged his thick shoulders. Finkel was going to his first finals.

With everyone at the event watching, Finkel crushed an Alaskan fisherman to win his first Pro Tour event ever, and a check for $25,000. Outside the Armory, fans closed in on Finkel. They all wanted him to sign their cards. They had a new nickname for him, too, not Stinkel, Wrinkle, or Tinkle, not Fro or Ronald McFinkel. They called him Finkeltron, the boy who played like a machine.

Finkel didn't just get a new moniker, he got a new team. Out from the crowd came Steve OMS and Williams, followed by Dave Price and the Dead Guys. Finkel had long admired the Dead Guys' tenacity and honesty, and now they were coming for him. "Hey, man," said Price warmly, "let's go out for a drink to celebrate."

Finkel smiled widely. It was a perfect moment, until he slipped his key into his car and it wouldn't start. The car was dead. For an instant, he felt like fate had reared its ugly head again. Maybe he couldn't escape his destiny after all. Maybe he would just be forever stalled.

But then his mom wandered over, and put her arm around his shoulder. "Don't worry, Jon," she said, softly. "I'll ride back with the tow truck. You just stay back and enjoy your win."

He did.

Winds of Change

Sorcery

Each player counts the cards in his or her hand, shuffles those cards into his or her deck, and then draws that many cards.
(When you play Winds of Change, it doesn't count as a card in your hand.)

Illus. Adam Rex

5. FINKELTRON

It was a hot summer day in 1998, and thousands of sports fans were following the lead of their favorite athletes: they were going to Disney World.

They stormed Disney's Wide World of Sports, a sprawling complex covering thousands of acres near the theme parks in Orlando, Florida. Wide-eyed Little Leaguers roamed the Baseball Quadraplex, four big fields outside the towering Cracker Jack stadium. Joggers pounded the wooded cross-country trails. Softball girls hurled balls around the Diamondplex, a meticulously manicured circle of four bright green fields.

On any given day, all-American kids might catch a glimpse of an all-American sports star: Shaq shooting hoops, Tiger Woods playing golf. On this day, they queued to meet an overweight twenty-year-old from New Jersey. His name was Jon Finkel or, as some now called him, the Michael Jordan of Magic.

The occasion was a special event for Magic's under-eighteen set, the so-called Juniors division. Finkel himself had started in the Juniors category, when he showed up at his first Magic tournament in New York in 1996. As part of this weekend's event, competitors would have a chance to recreationally challenge, or "gunsling," against some of the best over-eighteen Magic pros in the game. And, since wiping out his rival Jersey Kid to win $25,000 at the Pro Tour New York event, there was no one better than the Finkeltron.

Finkel was a star, and he was shining in Magic in every possible way. Depending on how high players placed, they received points that affected their overall ranking. With all his high finishes, Finkel finished the 1997–98 season with more points than anyone else. This earned him the coveted title Player of the Year. Most impressively, in the minds of the increasingly competitive Magic pros, Finkel had become the number one money earner in the game. In total, he had won $85,000 in less than two years. It sure beat minimum wage at Domino's.

Richard Garfield and the rest at Wizards of the Coast were vested in keeping Finkel's star on the rise. The aspirational marketing concept, modeled after tennis, had paid off. By elevating Magic to a sport, they spawned a network of competition that had saved the game from becoming a fad, and was now resulting in consistent revenues of nearly $125 million per year. Magic was now available in nine languages in fifty-two countries around the world.

From Boston to Bombay, brainy disenfranchised boys like Finkel had found a way to compete. Magic shops teemed with players working their way up Wizards' tournament system. It started at the neighborhood level, with Magic players dueling at their local courts, the Magic game shops. By now, there were nearly two thousand Magic tournaments each week. Becoming accomplished on the local level, players rose to the regional events. At qualifiers, they jockeyed to win the right to go to a Pro Tour event. If they made it there, they fought to reach the upper echelon at any given tournament—the Top 8.

From there, they competed at national events and, at the highest level, the World Championship.

If that wasn't enough to entice players, Wizards was raising the stakes. For Magic to be a real sport, Garfield and his colleagues mused, players had to be able to make a living at the game. They didn't just want hobbyists, they wanted Magic pros in the ultimate sense of the word. The best way to ensure that was to increase the booty. Wizards doubled the annual $1 million purse, distributed over a year of Magic tournaments, to $2 million.

Capping this off, Finkel's ascension had become a turning point for the game. The low stakes and bad reputations were replaced by high stakes and an impeccable star. Finkel didn't cheat or drink or throw his cards. Even when he lost, he was sportsmanlike, congratulating his opponent and shrugging off the loss as just one game. He seemed to implicitly understand that key for any professional cardplayer: short-term losses pale next to long-term gains.

Best of all, he was the kind of kid everyone could admire. Parents viewed him as the ultimate nice guy. Jocks saw him as a steadfast competitor. Even the most outcast kid on the fringe of town at a game store full of pariahs could relate to Finkel; he was, after all, one of them. If Finkel could be a star, then maybe they could, too. Players read about Finkel in *Sideboard,* Wizards' magazine, and critiqued his strategies online. He was even the subject of a feature story in his hometown newspaper, the *Star-Ledger:* " 'Magic' cards conjure cash teenager."

Finkel learned the extent of this devotion for the first time during the gunsling event at Disney's Wide World of Sports. All day, he and his friend Steve OMS, now also a formidable player, sat behind the card table signing Magic cards and playing hands with awestruck geeky kids. At one point, a young fat boy with horribly thick glasses waddled up and handed Finkel a card. "You're my hero," the boy squeaked.

Finkel eyed the kid, wondering if he heard him correctly. The boy just smiled, as he giddily snatched the signed card from Finkel's paw and ran off to show his mother.

"Maybe I should tell him to consider getting a different hero," Finkel said to Steve OMS, who chuckled beside him.

But Finkel wasn't joking around. Despite his success, Finkel hardly felt heroic. When he looked at himself in the mirror, he saw a failure, in mind and in body. He still felt, as he said, like a "loser" inside. After all his years of good grades and his near-perfect SAT score, what did he have to show for it? He had screwed up his shot at an Ivy League school. Then he managed to flunk out of the only university that accepted him, Rutgers. Meanwhile, his sister, Jenny, was up at Columbia. It was bad enough that his parents were now officially divorced; he was sure that his academic fiasco only compounded their disappointment.

Physically, things were worse than ever. On his twentieth birthday, he tipped the scale at over 250 pounds. One day he tried to button his pants, but couldn't. When he went to a store to get himself a new pair, they didn't have his size. "Maybe you should try the Big and Tall Men shop down the street," the cute girl behind the counter said. Finkel stomped outside. "Jesus," he said. "I am fat! I can't buy pants in a normal store! I mean, what the fuck?"

His attempt to distract people from his weight by bleaching his hair only made matters worse; now he was a fat guy in tent-sized pants with goofy thick glasses and a bad dye job. While other guys were dating and hooking up, Finkel felt like a hopeless eunuch. He was probably the only champion on the planet who couldn't get laid, he figured.

To compound his feelings of inadequacy, the spotlight was trained on him more than ever. As the new poster boy for Magic, Finkel was doing more and more personal appearances and television interviews. Despite the empathetic appeal that Finkel's underdog persona had with their target audience, the staff at Wizards did their best to help get their superstar into shape.

Skaff, the friend of Garfield's who dreamed up the Pro Tour, began holding Sunday-night basketball games at the end of tournament weekends. It became a ritual on the road; while the players were competing, Skaff would scour whatever town they were in—

Tokyo, Rome, Kuala Lumpur—for a basketball court. Then he'd herd out the most misfit Magic players—like a busload of rejects from the Bad News Bears—and nudge them out onto the pavement. These guys had spent most of their lives being the last in the lineup at school, and now, for once, they were going to learn how to play.

During one game, Finkel got the ball and charged awkwardly for the basket. Just as he leapt, he got checked in the chest, falling forward, and watched in slow motion as his glasses flew from his face and shattered on the ground. As the laughter swelled around him once again, he knew what he had to do. Now that he had become a world champion, he had better start acting like one. Cue the Rocky theme song. It was time for a change.

Just before midnight, the trouble set in.

It was fast approaching the end of the second day of a Magic tournament being held at the Meadowlands in East Rutherford, New Jersey. Ordinarily home to the Nets basketball team or Devils hockey pros, the arena had been outfitted with card tables and dragon banners to accommodate the rounder and spindlier competitors who gathered this weekend. With the ESPN2 crew arriving the next day to interview the tournament winner, Skaff and the other representatives from Wizards were anxious to see which player would be under the spotlight. As a chubby player in baggy pants leapt up from a table with a triumphant snort, Skaff drew a long slow breath. "Okay," he sighed, rubbing his palms together, "it's Zvi."

The exceptionally bright and idiosyncratic son of two biochemists, twenty-year-old Columbia University math student Zvi Mowshowitz made Finkel look like Tom Cruise. As one Magic scribe described him, Zvi was a "giggling, unshaven madman" known for his cocky play, hyenalike laugh, and seemingly total disregard for his appearance. Zvi would show up at Magic events with perpetual bedhead and a beard as patchy as a neglected Chia Pet. If he was going to take home this tournament and represent the sport on TV, Skaff thought, they'd better clean him up before morning.

There was one problem: where to find a good barber at midnight in New Jersey. One Wizards guy had an idea. He told Skaff he had a couple of cousins living not too far away in Brighton Beach who worked in a beauty shop. Maybe he could phone them and ask them to drive to the Meadowlands now for an emergency house call. "Call them!" Skaff said.

The next thing they knew, inside the arena, Zvi was snorting and giggling loudly in a folding chair at one a.m. as two sexy Russian women snipped away at his hair and lathered his face. As it turned out the next day, he didn't take home the grand prize, but as he stood smiling on the stage with his third-place plaque, he sure looked good.

Zvi wasn't the only Magic makeover. Since that fateful day on the basketball court, Finkel was now spending his tournament winnings on sprucing himself up. He bought contact lenses. He went to the mall, and spent a couple of thousand dollars on new clothes: button-up shirts, new jeans. He ditched his old broken-down car, and bought a brand-new Saturn. He invested in mutual funds. He joined a gym, replaced Happy Meals with tuna sandwiches, and began working out four days a week.

Most dramatically of all, he committed himself to becoming a student again. After flunking out in the spring of 1997, he reenrolled at Rutgers in the fall of 1998, telling his parents that he was going to use his Magic winnings to pay for his entire college education himself. They were thrilled—not so much that he was footing the bill, but that he was going back to school at all. By now they had resigned themselves to letting Jon call his own shots. And though they held out hope that he would stick with school, they couldn't count on it. Finkel, like many of his Magic friends, seemed to feel almost boxed in by college. Having had a taste of money and independence, they were even less inclined to spend a life working for someone else.

But, in reality, Finkel had yet to make up his mind. Though he was making plenty of money at Magic, he didn't dream he could be a cardplayer for the rest of his life. There was one world in which he thought he could apply his gamesmanship and analytical skills: Wall Street. Being a trader relied on the same traits as a good card-player's—intelligence, confidence, decisiveness, and the ability to live with bad decisions along the way. He declared his major: economics.

On campus, he did his best to fit in with the other students. His roommates, like him, were hard-core Philadelphia Eagles fans, and the group would stay up late watching games and talking sports. Finkel, who had been advised by his mother long ago to play down his smarts, rarely brought up his double life as a Magic champ. It was only after someone inquired about his frequent weekend trips that he would discuss it.

"You know Magic," he'd explain, "it's nerdy. You always see three overweight guys in the corner playing this game." When girls were around, he experienced what he was sure every Magic player, no matter how accomplished, felt at one time or another: embarrassment.

But if he could help it, he wouldn't be embarrassed for long. Now that he was transforming himself in so many other ways, he decided it was time to enter what he felt was the most challenging game of all: dating. Though he had lost his virginity on a drunken one-night stand the year before, that was the extent of his love life. After all those years being beaten up and picked on at school, he barely had any confidence in dealing with girls. Some of his Magic buddies, like David Williams and Dave Price, seemed to have no problem with women; they were smooth, conversational, confident. But Finkel felt ill-equipped. Sure, he could wield a Lava Axe like a wizard, but how many women would be impressed by that? If he was going to conquer his fear, he knew, he needed some help. And like a lot of guys in the late 1990s, he found it online.

PickUpGuide.com was one of many sites devoted to helping guys beat the game of love. On the top of the homepage was a quote from Robert Kennedy: "Only those who dare to fail greatly can achieve greatly." Finkel read on: "If you are a 'nice guy,' and have not been successful with women up to now, then prepare to be awakened, as the solutions await you in these pages!"

The site was run by a guy named Maniac who "lives in Tokyo and likes to pick up chicks." Its systematic approach to a complex problem spoke to Finkel on a deep and instinctive level. The site featured rules to follow, strategies to employ, just like a rule book for Dungeons and Dragons or Magic. Finkel was ready to play.

At night after class, he'd hunch over his computer and read up on all the advice. The problem, he learned, was that he was, as the site put it in one of its numerous acronyms, an AFC, or Average Frustrated Chump. Maniac defined an AFC as "a 'nice guy' who has no pick up skills and rarely manages to close a target pick up. Also a guy who tends to supplicate in his behavior to HBs [Hot Babes]. Meaning, buying flowers for a chick when going out for coffee, putting her on a pedestal, and generally letting women walk all over him in the vein [sic] hope of somehow being seen as attractive in their eyes."

To win over the HBs, Finkel read, he had to transform himself from an AFC to a PUA, a Pick Up Artist. This meant developing the techniques in his "toolbox" to overcome obstacles such as ASD, "Anti-Slut Defense—The chick logic a woman (especially younger ones) will go through to relieve the guilt from having sex too quickly with a man"; or the Anti-AI, "Anti Approach Invitation—Unconscious actions by an HB to do everything to avoid your specific attention. Walking away from you, avoiding EC [eye contact], creating a cockblock scenario, etc."

Finkel would have to proceed slowly, plying his trade in clubs, which Maniac referred to as "boot camp." Inside, he could exercise techniques such as "Kino," or the kinesthetic approach, "physical touch to get a woman in a state of approval or arousal." Like a poker player, he would learn to spot a woman's tells. Maniac called these AI for Approach Invitations—"Unconscious actions by an HB to get your specific attention . . . dropping something in front of you, asking you a question, fumbling with something in front of you, making nervous gestures."

After weeks of research, Finkel knew it was time to put his techniques into play. If he could become the best in the world at Magic, he figured, why not this? Maybe he could be not just a PUA, but a

PUG, a Pick Up Guru, or a PUM, a Pick Up Master. He slipped in his contacts, buttoned up his shirt, and hit the road.

Near a bus stop, he found an HB, a hot babe in a tight black sweater, waiting for her ride. Finkel snapped into action. His mind raced over the plays he'd memorized from the site. Should he whip out some Neuro Linguistic Programming, planting a suggestion in her mind ("imagine you're dating a guy like me, and we're out for a fancy dinner...")? Should he try some swift Kino? The moves flashed by like playing cards. No, he knew, this called for the 3 Second Rule.

"You should immediately try to meet a woman within 3 seconds of seeing her (or her seeing you)," Maniac wrote, " 'DO NOT HESITATE.' Any hesitation will give you more time to falter and come up with fear-based excuses in your mind. It will also give your target time to think negatively about you."

Without thinking, Finkel marched forward. "What time is it?" he said.

The blonde checked her watch. "About five," she said, smiling.

"Thanks," Finkel said. He stood silently. The site had told him to talk to a woman within three seconds, but then what? After a few awkward moments, Finkel turned on his heels and went on his way.

Compared to this game, Magic was easy.

The Hustler by Walter Tevis was the book that broke the floodgates open. Middle-class America knew nothing of the atmosphere which lurked within the American institution known as the Pool Hall before Tevis' book openly addressed its subculture of deviants, hustlers, players, and otherwise shady individuals. It mythologized the smoky rooms filled with miscreants, men some described as losers, dreamers, men whose lives others from the outside accused of being wasted largely due to the incredible number of hours spent playing on green velvet. These men viewed their lives differently, but to the outside world, the pool hall was a den of evil.

Pool halls were also notorious for a reason that doesn't hold true today: They were nearly completely absent women. Time at the Pool Hall was time away from the house, away from the wife, away from a thousand responsibilities. This was part of its lure. The pool hall was a self-contained universe, operating on its own laws, where the value system of the white middle class was ignored. . . . Until recently there was no comparable place in American life.

Magic: The Gathering is played by people all over the world who only dimly know that there is such a thing as the Pro Tour. Even people who qualify regularly for events may not know about what pro players do when the tournament has long been over, or when the field is reduced to eight. The casual observer may never notice where most of the Pro Tour players are come sundown. You may need to look in cafeterias, in bars, in hotel lobbies. You may need to stay awake well into the midnight hours. You may have to search high and low to find that Mecca of modern magic, the modern pool hall that is the Pro Tour money game circuit . . . yes brother, come on down to the greatest show on Magic earth, the Pro Tour money game.

The essay, "The New Pool Halls: Gambling and Magic," was becoming the talk of Magic groups on the Internet. Written by Brian Hacker, a blue-haired player from the University of California, San Diego, it revealed what the elite pro players had come to regard as a highlight of any tournament: the money games.

While Wizards was now dangling a multimillion-dollar purse for the top players, hoping to spawn professionals who could make a living at the game, the players began growing up and raising the stakes on their own. As player Bob Maher put it, "If you start throwing that much money at twenty-one-year-olds, they start experimenting; they try to figure out what they really enjoy." And what the card shark kids found they liked most was gambling.

It started, as Hacker noted, in the lobbies and back halls of tournaments, long after the official play had ceased. Players anted up $50 each, and competed, often in teams of three-on-three, for the best out of nine games. The winners got the other teams' money—and their cards. At three in the morning in a hotel lobby, players would be screaming, smoking, windmilling their cards on the table. Cash changed hands, beers were poured. In no small way, these clandestine Magic games began to resemble the scene of poker rooms, but with much younger players.

Though Wizards didn't endorse the money drafting, they didn't ban it either. "Officially we don't know about it," Skaff said, but he was happy to see it flourish. If you're going to have a game that was really a sport, he thought, you needed wagering to happen. People play chess for money. People play golf for money. "If people aren't putting up money," he said, "then it's not a sport. We want players to think it's a game worthy of betting on."

As far as Garfield was concerned, wagering improved the meta-game—the context in which the game is played—and, thus, the game itself. "There's nothing more compelling than the meta-game of money," he said. "It's so easy to score. And it's so fluid. If you're playing for matchsticks, you never know who's the best, you just don't care. But, in the end, if you're playing well, you'll have money instead of matchsticks. It's a way of making people play the game seriously." Players appreciated it for just this reason. "You want to make that guy reach into his wallet and pull out something and hand it to you," said Randy Buehler, one of the players from CMU, the Carnegie Mellon team.

Some had a more difficult time parting with their cash than others. As the money-drafting scene built, one of the most competitive players proved to be Finkel's young buddy from Texas, David Williams. When the two first met, Williams was still the newbie gamer looking up to Finkel for advice and struggling to find his place on Magic's Pro Tour. Though nowhere near as accomplished, Williams followed Finkel's lead and aggressively insinuated himself into the scene.

When he wasn't officially competing, Williams was hopping between the ever-present side games at the tournaments. At home, he would play Magic online. Like Finkel, he was intuitive and something of a raw talent. But as Finkel soon noticed, they differed in one crucial way: Williams went on tilt.

This became clear during one money draft game between Finkel and Randy Buehler. Buehler, a doctoral student, was sometimes called a "rules lawyer" for his conservative sense of gaming. Finkel was playing with Williams on his team. When Finkel dramatically windmilled down a card to claim victory, Williams leapt up to high-five his friend. It wasn't the measly $50 that mattered, it was the win, and, as Finkel observed, Williams couldn't get enough of that winning feeling.

But amid the cheers, Buehler raised his hand. He questioned a small detail of play that, if enforced, would negate Finkel's win. Though Finkel was learning to take such inevitable bumps in stride, Williams was incensed. How dare Buehler try to spoil their victory? After some discussion, however, Finkel agreed, much to Williams's consternation, to a do-over with Buehler. This time, Finkel lost. And Williams, who had bet on the game against Buehler, refused to pay; it would be months before he would finally fork over the cash.

"You don't need to get all emotional about it," Finkel told Williams after the game.

Williams just lowered his head.

"Dude," Finkel continued, "what are you going to do? You lose sometimes. We're not playing chess here. You're not going to win every time."

Williams said he knew, but, as Finkel watched him walk away with slumped shoulders, he doubted that his friend meant it.

With all the cash flowing in from tournaments and money games, Magic players began spending like high rollers. Wizards was now hosting events in more and more exotic locales: Oslo, Manila, Kyoto, Madrid. Expensive steak dinners became ritual on the tourney circuit. Foreigners didn't know what to make of the motley crew of baseball-capped young men sauntering into the restaurants and ordering the most expensive wines. When asked, they just introduced themselves as cardplayers. People assumed they meant poker.

After dinner, the Magic geeks might go to a strip club, blowing $2,000 in a night. Other times, they made often feeble attempts to pick up women on their own. One night in China, a group of players went out to what they thought was a standard bar. Skaff, the Pro Tour organizer at Wizards, could see that it was a human experiment in the making. "It's like you carefully sifted and selected the nerdiest people from four continents and threw them into Hong Kong nightlife," he said.

The group huddled in a corner, turtling into their shirts, and nursing their beers. When a woman in a slinky black dress asked one of them to dance, he gladly accepted and made his way to the dance floor. But the other players thought the woman had fairly thick ankles. At the bar, Skaff inquired about the place, which turned out to be something like a brothel. "If a madam says that a woman wants to dance with you, then that woman is female," explained the bartender, "but if a woman comes up to you and asks to dance, well, she's a man." The Magic player disappearing with the transvestite on the dance floor didn't seem to mind.

With the players becoming players in the real sense, the cliques began taking on new shape. Gone were the punky Jersey Kids and the old Pacific Coast Legends. In their place were universally acceptable cool characters like Williams and Dave Price's clan, the Dead Guys. Since Finkel's big win in New York, he had started rolling more frequently with Dave Price and the Dead Guys crew. They admired not only his ability but his honesty—the fact that, like them, he won his events fair and square.

Price, who was a couple of years older than Finkel, became a surrogate big brother. Hip, literate, and into punk rock, he was an edgier version of Finkeltron, known around the tournament scene as King of Beatdown, because of his track record for dominating Magic qualifying events. Finkel began rooming with Price on the road, swilling beers while Price regaled him with Kerouac and Bukowski.

Finkel, a lifelong reader himself, credited reading with making him a better cardplayer. "The idea of literature is about making connections," he said, "and that's what intuition is." At Rutgers, he had been taking literature courses, which refined his analytical thinking. He transposed his learning into the language of playing cards—

looking ahead at his future moves, deducing the best plays, intuiting what was in the other players' hands.

In between Magic tournaments, Finkel, sometimes accompanied by David Williams, who was now studying electrical engineering at Princeton, would drive up to stay with Price and the Dead Guys at Cornell. There, they put the mastermind principle into play. Late into the night around the kitchen table of someone's apartment, they constructed the ultimate decks with which they could compete on the road. They found an edge in collaboration, working together on strategies and techniques. With so many bright players—Ivy League students, doctoral candidates—it was like having the best cardplaying think tank on the planet.

Finkel's game had never been better. As he continued to dominate on the road, he slowly transformed himself. He dressed better. He lost weight. And, after months of working on his pickup-guide techniques, he even hooked up.

It happened one night at Rutgers. He had been out drinking with some friends and ran into a couple of girls. Finkel, the Average Frustrated Chump, whipped out the advance techniques: the 3 Second Rule, followed by a little Kino, and a play on her obvious Approach Invitations. The next thing he knew, he was stumbling back with one of the girls to her apartment. He hadn't arrived there by lying or cheating or posing. He had just behaved as a more outgoing and confident version of himself.

Though he never considered himself completely happy, Finkel felt that, at long last, he was in control of his game. He was doing well in school, winning tens of thousands of dollars playing cards, making great friends. He was shedding all the old weight from the past. He was even getting laid. Soon he was going to see the movie that all the Magic players were talking about, *Rounders*.

Finkel was intrigued by the movie's tagline, which he'd seen in ads: "In the Game of Life . . . Play the Cards You're Dealt." The story follows a young law student, played by Matt Damon, who's recovering after losing his tuition in a high-stakes poker game. When his old cardplaying buddy, played by Ed Norton, gets out of prison and needs to pay off a big loss to a Russian lowlife, Damon crawls back into the world of underground poker.

Sitting in the dark theater that night, Finkel watched the action in a trance. There was nothing glamorous about the portrayal of the poker world in *Rounders,* but it was compelling nonetheless. Finkel loved the reality the movie portrayed. It was mental competition for money, he thought. Here was this young kid playing cards obsessively, winning enough cash to pay his way through college. The more he played, the more he transformed, discovering himself, his values, his life.

As the credits rolled, Finkel couldn't move from his seat. A lightning bolt shot from the screen through his freshly bleached Jewfro and electrified his brain.

Holy shit, he realized, that's me.

He had to find a poker game, and fast.

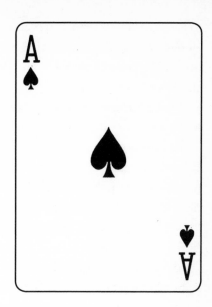

6. ROUNDERS

Hungry seagulls cawed on the boardwalk as the sun peered over the horizon like a bloodshot eye. It was a typical morning in Atlantic City, New Jersey—AC. Prostitutes in gold lamé wobbled from the casinos in towering, translucent heels. Jitney buses creaked down roads like postapocalyptic ice-cream trucks converted for human cargo. Blue-haired ladies with plastic buckets of change headed inside the buildings to scour for slots.

Deep inside the parking garage of Trump's Taj Mahal Hotel and Casino, another gambler's day had just begun. Finkel rose from the seat of his car and stretched his arms with a yawn. It was time to play poker again.

It didn't take long after he saw *Rounders* for Finkel to become obsessed. Just as he had once crashed on the benches at Penn Station to game around the clock at Neutral Ground, Finkel was now pulling all-nighters in AC. Ever thrifty, he chose to spend nights in his Saturn rather than blow $100 on a crappy room. He'd rather spend every cent he had on his game.

Prior to *Rounders,* Finkel, underage at twenty, had never set foot inside a casino or played a serious hand of Hold 'Em or Seven Card Stud. The closest he came to Atlantic City was a Monopoly board. But he was ready to set cash in for real. Though he had made more than $100,000 playing Magic, he was starting to lose interest in his old game. He needed a new challenge to spark his passions. The more he learned about Texas Hold 'Em poker, the more that game fit the bill.

Before coming to Atlantic City, Finkel academically studied the rules of the game online. Compared to Magic, Hold 'Em seemed fairly straightforward. The object is to make the best poker hand using a combination of five cards on the table. Before the cards are dealt from a standard fifty-two-card deck, the player to the left of the dealer opens with a bet of half the designated minimum. This is known as the small blind, because the player is betting without the benefit of seeing his cards. The next player to the left bets the full minimum, known as the big blind.

After the blinds, each player is dealt two cards, facedown, known as the hole cards. The player to the left of the big blind starts the play by either calling, raising, or folding. In so-called limit Hold 'Em games, players must bet in designated increments; in no-limit, players can push in all their chips. After everyone's bet, the dealer discards, or "burns," one more card, then peels off three communal cards, faceup, called the flop. Another round of betting occurs. Then comes the fourth card, called the turn or fourth street, and another round of bets. Finally, the last communal card, called the river or fifth street, is dealt, followed by one last round of bets. The player who makes the best hand wins.

Since Hold 'Em hit casinos in the mid-1960s, it has became the most popular poker variation, as well as the featured event of the

World Series of Poker in Las Vegas. It achieved this status by combining the classic recipe of game design—easy to play, difficult to master—with an adrenaline-producing amount of wagering. While anyone can get in on a game, the variety of potential players and play make it tantalizingly complex. Doyle Brunson, the champion player, once described it as "the most fascinating of all the various forms of Poker." It's also the most seductive. With the right cards, anyone can win a particular hand. But, in the long run, the players with the most skills win.

As Finkel headed inside the casino, he just hoped he'd be able to prove himself before they threw him out for being a kid. The moment he heard the bells of the slots and the plastic riffle of chips his blood began to race. Over in the poker room, rows of card tables were lined up under the gaudy lights, with players hunched over the green felt. Waitresses in miniskirts carried trays of drinks. The room smelled of stale booze and cigarettes. Finkel felt for the $500 roll of cash in his pocket, and gave his initials to a mustached guy behind a counter, who added JSF to the $10/$20-limit Texas Hold 'Em list.

Sipping a coffee, Finkel systematically examined the arena. Though this was a new environment, he felt at ease. It was just another card room after all. Sure, there were no dragons on the wall or silvery Magic wrappers on the floor, but, other than that, it was like a grown-up version of the Realms or the Ground. Only the faces had changed. Instead of scrappy teens like Williams or Steve OMS or the Dead Guys, Finkel looked into the liquid eyes of weathered old men and tourists in tropical pants. But they were gamers all the same.

Sizing up his competition, Finkel could feel the edge sharpen within him. Compared to him, after all, the average poker player came to cash games late. He had been playing cards competitively since age sixteen. Magic had been his boot camp. He had traveled the world, developed both the mental and physical stamina for competition, a knack for keeping his head cool even during the worst losses. In poker parlance, he never went "on tilt"; he knew how to manage his emotions.

"You've got to have the emotional understanding that you can make the right play time and time again," he would say, "but you can still lose. And even if you lose four times in a row, you're still supposed to make the same play the fifth time. It's a very easy concept in theory, but in practice it's much harder, especially when you see people making bad moves and they win. You have to do the right move all the time."

Once called to join the game, Finkel put his training into play. Here he was at a table, feeling the smooth cards in his hand, just like Magic. Cards flipped, he bet, he folded, and his stacks of chips began to build. By the end of the day, Finkel left up $500. Cashing out his chips, he walked outside only to see that night had come. He climbed into his car, lowered the seat, and went to sleep. When the sun came up, he started playing again.

The trips to Atlantic City became more frequent. He'd go on weekends as well as during the week. He didn't drink or go to strip clubs or take in a show. He came to play, and learn. But it wasn't always easy. After that first day, Finkel realized that even the skills and stamina he had refined through Magic couldn't substitute for experience. He practiced his overarching strategy from Magic: to always make the right play, even when you're losing.

But poker wasn't just a science, it was an art. To succeed, a player also had to have the ability to read opponents and use intuition. Finkel simply wasn't seasoned enough in poker to find his way through such intricacies or, for that matter, identify what the right play in a given situation might be. Within a few months, he had dropped $10,000. He needed guidance.

One day at a table, he found himself sitting next to a seedy guy in a navy blue jumpsuit. The man was heavy and unkempt, with hair sticking up in several directions. Despite his appearance, however, he was the talk of the room. Finkel heard he'd won a few million bucks in his day. The guy was cocky, but in a shallow way. Finkel had a name for such an attitude: he called it the Arrogant Idiot Complex. He had seen it infest Magic players, guys who were good at one thing to the exclusion of everything else. But Finkel was never one to turn down an opportunity to learn, a mistake he'd seen many players make. Even an Arrogant Idiot had something to teach him.

"Hey," Finkel said. "I really want to get good at poker. I really want to make money at it. You have any advice you can give me?"

The guy looked at Finkel, this kid, and chuckled. Finkel was sure he thought he was a fool. "Sure, kid," he replied, "read *Hold 'Em Poker for Advanced Players* by David Sklansky and Mason Malmuth. It'll cost you twenty-five bucks but it will pay for itself every time you sit down at a poker table."

"Thanks," Finkel said. "What's your name?"

"They call me the Wizard," he said, then walked away. Some things, Finkel thought, are meant to be.

Finkel beelined for the Gambler's Book Shop, a store near the Taj. He couldn't believe his eyes: rows and rows of books, magazines, pamphlets. Compared to a relatively new game like Magic, poker had an ancient history and a canon of literature. Finkel devoured it.

Back in his dorm room, while his roommates studied calculus and astronomy, Finkel pored over the Wizard's recommended tome. The book, written by a couple of trained mathematicians, broke down all the essential strategies from position (how to bet based on where you're sitting at the table) to slow-playing (luring players into the pot when you have a good hand). At night, Finkel wrestled with the questions at the back of the book, covering the answers with one hand and testing his skills:

"When is it correct to bet two overcards?" Finkel muttered, "Frequently, especially if you have a backdoor flush potential."

"What type of hand should you bet on fourth street?" He said, "Hands that, if already beaten, have no outs."

If this had been the SAT, he would have scored another 1550. On weekends, he'd make the long journey to AC to put the strategies into practice. But the drives began to wear him down. One night, at his usual table at the Taj, a sympathetic player suggested he check out turf closer to home. "You ever play at clubs in New York?" the guy asked.

"No," Finkel said. "I'm not aware of them."

The guy scribbled a name on the back of a business card and handed it to the kid.

"What's the Diamond?" Finkel said.

You are walking down a dark city street. It's nighttime. You come to a red door on the side of a run-down building. You hear a motor spin, and look up to see a camera facing down at you. The intercom crackles. What do you do?

As Finkel stood in front of the door late one night in New York City, it felt like a scene from a Dungeons and Dragons game. But that's exactly how his life seemed to play out. Marshall McLuhan, the media scholar, once wrote that "games are dramatic models of our psychological lives providing release of particular tensions . . . the games of a people reveal a great deal about them." As long as he could remember, Finkel had always been revealed by his games.

As a kid, D&D taught him to explore his imagination and develop his heroic attributes. In England, the live-action role-playing games let him express these ideas in person. As a teenager, Magic rewarded his inherent analytical and strategic skills with fame and fortune, nurturing his confidence. Now his adventure into the world of poker had led him to this paint-chipped doorway on Twentieth Street between Fifth and Sixth Avenues in New York City. And as he buzzed the intercom, he had no idea where this journey would lead.

"Hi," he said, looking up into the smudgy lens. "This guy gave me this card. I'd like to play some." Finkel held the card up to the camera, which stared indifferently. Finkel heard this club had been the basis for one of the poker rooms in *Rounders*. From what he gathered, underground poker clubs like this one existed in something of a gray area. Technically, gambling was illegal, but by charging a small "membership" fee, clubs could run poker games just like one might find in the back of a social hall. The door buzzed, and he stepped inside.

Climbing up the steps, he came to a paint-chipped door with a grated window. Another camera stared down. A towering guy with fiery red hair stepped up and gave Finkel the once-over. Though he had shed much of his bulk and lost the doughy baby fat, Finkel still looked underage, particularly with his badly dyed blond Jewfro. Finkel handed him the business card, and the guy squinted at the name. "Fill this out," the guy grunted, sliding a membership form under the grate.

Since casinos required players to be twenty-one to gamble, Finkel hesitated to put his real birthday on the membership form. Still twenty, he didn't want to get thrown out after having come this far. But after he scribbled his correct age, no one cared. His cash was as good as everyone else's, and they happily slid over a rack of chips.

As he stepped inside, the Diamond Club smelled like a giant ashtray, and sort of resembled one, too. The tiny loft had filthy brick walls with cobwebbed pipes exposed like monster bones. A soda machine with cracked glass buzzed too loudly in a corner. A few plants wilted as though they hadn't been watered in weeks, and gasped in the cigarette clouds. Two bookshelves were inexplicably stacked with dozens of copies of the same book: *The Greatest Jewish Athletes of All Time.*

But, as Finkel could clearly see, no one here came expecting the tacky splendor of an Atlantic City casino. These were hard-core gamers—just like him. It was like a poker version of Neutral Ground. About fifty players hunched around fifteen tables, stacked with cards and chips. Unlike the nerdy kids who swarmed to Magic, poker drew an older crowd plucked from seemingly every urban faction. Fat cabbies gnawed pepperoni pizza. Wall Street brokers riffled chips in sharp business suits. A long-bearded Orthodox Jew fidgeted with his yarmulke.

Finkel tried his best to be cool, as he stood there with his small tray of chips. But he was startled to hear someone calling his name. "Hey, Jon!" came the voice. Finkel turned around to see a young guy, slightly balding, with dark hair and glasses and a loud Hawaiian shirt. "Jon Finkel!" the guy repeated, "I thought it was you." Finkel knew exactly who this was: Mike May.

Mike was an occasional part of the Neutral Ground crowd, an exceptionally polite but somewhat neurotic Magic player who, while decent, never got into the Pro Tour scene. Though smart, like a lot of the Ground's card sharks, twenty-seven-year-old Mike had trouble finding his way in the outside world. He had been drifting between menial jobs around New York, from working as a bike messenger to interviewing patients about their bowel movements for drug companies. Now, he told Finkel, he had finally found his life's vocation—playing poker.

For the past couple of years, Mike had been eking out a living at the game both here and uptown at a fancier place called the Mayfair, another inspiration for the clubs in *Rounders*. The Mayfair was the more upscale place, home to higher-stakes Hold 'Em games featuring $1,000 no-limit buy-ins and limit games of $75/$150 or $100/$200. Mike preferred the Diamond, where the stakes were lower but the potential return was high. He also liked the management.

The club was run by a couple of colorful Irish brothers who had opened it a couple of years before. The older brother was a personable entrepreneur who used to run dance clubs in Houston, and was a fan of theme restaurants—country and western bars, sci-fi theaters, the more fog machines and neon the better. He tried to dress up the Diamond Club as best he could—thus the bookshelves, which he lined with hardcovers bought in bulk at the Strand down on Broadway and Twelfth.

The younger brother, Mike said, was a loose cannon. "If you took Mr. T and made him a white Irish guy who had been thrown out of the marines for violent tendencies and was gay and liked young Asian men, you'd have this guy," Mike explained. But aside from their occasional shouting matches when they played cards, the Irish brothers ran a tight ship.

The Diamond brothers understood the grind of a professional poker player's life, Mike said, and always made sure this was a good place to do business. Smart players could earn about $40 per hour playing $10/$20 limit games and the crowd was more, as he said, "proletariat." In other words, there were plenty of fish, inexperienced players, who swam into this sea.

"You know," Mike told Finkel, "poker is amazingly simplistic compared to Magic. You've got a fifty-two-card deck; in Magic, you've got thousands of cards. In poker, you're playing individual hands, which don't have much cumulative effect on each other. In Hold 'Em, I'm dealt two cards. In Magic, I'm dealt seven and as I develop, each decision I make will have ramifications down the road. In poker, I have two aces. I move in. I win the pot. That's it. You can teach a monkey or computer program to execute it."

Finkel chuckled loudly, eliciting a sneer from a sweaty player at a table trying to concentrate on his hand. "Who's the kid?" the sweaty guy asked.

"You gotta watch out for Jon Finkel," Mike replied. "He's the Michael Jordan of Magic."

"Magic?" the guy scoffed. "Never heard of it."

"It's a game, like chess with cards. Finkel won over $100,000 on Magic freerolls," Mike explained. Freerolls was poker parlance for tourneys that didn't require buy-in fees. The sweaty guy raised his eyebrows, impressed. A professional poker player might not see that kind of return for a couple of years. "You know, Jon," Mike said, quietly, "as a Magic player, you're coming from a complicated game to a much more simplistic game in poker. You're taking a step down."

Finkel knew implicitly what he meant. If Magic had helped an amateur player like Mike find the edge in poker, imagine what a champ like Finkel could do.

Just like Neutral Ground, Outer Realms, and Fun and Games, the Diamond Club became Finkel's new home. He wanted to be the next Jedi of planet poker and his Obi-Wan was Mike or, as he was better known around these parts, Hollywood Mike.

Poker players, Finkel learned, behaved a lot like gamers in one other respect, too: they loved nicknames. Like Finkel, Mike was the sort of guy who had endured annoying nicknames over the years. For a while, he tried to pull off the virtually impossible feat of nicknaming himself—a direct violation of guy-code if ever there was one. But his suggestion—The Claw—didn't stick, no matter how hard he tried. Neither did the more feeble Dr. Polite, which a Magic player suggested. When a guy at the Diamond observed Mike's penchant for wearing tropical shirts, he dubbed him Hollywood.

Though Mike disliked the moniker, it did come in handy for one simple reason, he thought: it made him look like an ass. In fact, the whole reason he wore the Hawaiian shirts in the first place was to make players think he was a sucker. "If they think you're an idiot," he said, "they'll play differently against you. Some people go to great lengths to look loud and stupid, to look like you don't know what you're doing to make people go against you. I know people who are phenomenal at getting people to think they're giving up action, even though they're stone-cold killers."

It was all part of poker's necessary meta-game, the game beyond the cards. As in Magic, Mike said, anyone who spends enough time studying, enough time with the books, can master the game to some degree. You learn about things like the importance of position—how you're at a greater advantage the farther you are from the dealer—or the hierarchy of playable hole cards. That was all kid's stuff. The real differentiations broke off at a higher level, the nonintuitives. And around the Diamond Club, Mike said, one of the most important skills to master was game selection.

In the club's Hold 'Em matches, for example, there were generally ten players per table. Initially, Finkel's instinct was to just jump right in wherever he saw an empty seat. In the Magic world, after all, he had developed the confidence to take on anyone, anytime. But to succeed in poker, Mike explained, he had to be more discerning about which players he chose to challenge. "The more you know about the players' strengths and weaknesses, the greater your advantage," he said one afternoon at the club. "Let me show you what I mean."

Finkel followed Mike as they walked slowly around the room. "That's Tall Timmy," Mike said, lifting his chin toward a lanky, pony-tailed guy riffling his chips at one table. "Sometimes they call him Slow Timmy. He's a right-wing, pro-Bush vegetarian bookie. He's a good player. Don't give him a penny."

Finkel nodded.

"The guy next to him," Mike continued, pointing to a balding hip-ster in black horn-rimmed glasses and a paint-speckled jean jacket, "that's Nervous Noah. He's an artist. Lives downtown. He's paying off his art school loans. His hands tend to shake when he makes his bets. He hates his nickname. He's trying to eradicate it, but hasn't suc-ceeded yet. He's also a good player. Don't give him a penny."

They walked past the broken soda machine. "That guy in the yarmulke over there," Mike said, "that's Barry. He's a good player but has a large tilt factor. If he gets psychologically off balance, he'll lose everything he has. The guy next to him, Joe G," Mike said, pointing to a young Latino guy with a Yankees baseball cap, "excellent player, but he has an ego thing; if you challenge him, he'll feel he has to come back and he'll do things wrong. So, that's the kind of stuff you learn about the good players. But what about the others?"

Finkel shrugged.

"You don't want to sit in on a game where they're intelligently ag-gressive, raising a lot, putting pressure on you. You want to find the ones who are putting pressure on you but don't understand the game. They're the guys who are overly aggressive in play but not in-telligently aggressive. You're looking for what we call cowboys."

Cowboys, however, didn't necessarily come in ten-gallon hats. Mike pointed Finkel to a table in the corner under a clanking air conditioner. "You're looking for cosmetic things," Mike said, "maybe guys with gold teeth, maybe they don't care so much about the money. Guys in a business suit, that implies a certain something. That guy in the Foxwoods baseball cap and Taj T-shirt and sun-glasses, you know how he plays; he's tight, he's a rock. If a guy's got the nickname Doc, generally that's good. Guy's got a cowboy hat, generally that's good unless he's from Texas, where they know how to play Hold 'Em."

The two of them came to a corner in the back. Finkel reached into his pocket and took out a pack of cigarettes. He had recently picked up the habit. Taking a deep drag, he soaked in the stuff Mike had to teach him. It worked around his brain with the smoke.

Ultimately, Mike said, poker is also a game requiring enormous patience. As all the books explained, less than 30 percent of your hole cards are worth playing. The rest of the time you just have to fold. That required even more discipline than Magic.

"In Magic, you could leverage more skill," Mike said. "If you're a strong player playing a weak player, you tend to come up from above. But in poker, it's more a matter of playing your best game and riding out the wave. That's very difficult for a new player to understand. You have to always make the right move, even when the right move results in losing hands. To do something exactly correct over and over again and be punished for that has a very strange psychological effect.

"There are some nights where you can play perfect poker, and every gutshot straight that they draw for will get there, every flush will get there, every overpair you have will get cracked by a pair of threes. And you eventually feel that the universe hates you. It's very tough. That's a hard pain to describe." Mike paused. "You're not playing against ten players," he concluded. "You're playing against yourself."

As Finkel took a long drag of his smoke, Mike's words stirred his memories. Like a lot of smart misfit boys, he had grown up feeling as if the universe hated him. He tried to make all the right moves, but just got punished in return. As a result, he learned to keep his head down, and keep a poker face no matter how much he hurt inside. Now he brought that face here to this arena where the pain was a commodity, not a liability. His pain made him strong.

The armored car rolled through the night carrying its million-dollar booty. In the back wasn't gold or jewelry or cash. There were cardboard boxes from Wizards of the Coast, filled with the hottest new card game on the planet: Pokemon. Just as Magic's biggest star was discovering his bite, Wizards was seeding a new generation of card shark kids.

Originally released in Japan in 1998, Pokemon was based on an insanely popular Nintendo Game Boy game and television show about a legion of brightly colored "pocket monsters," or Pokemon, for short. Similar to Magic, players duel and trade cards, each of which corresponds to a uniquely powered creature—say, strong or meek, stinky or bashful. The object is to collect and "train" the creatures, a mission of no small psychological import to the target market of kids under twelve. For players, it's all about identifying their monstrous emotions, harnessing their power, or keeping them in check.

At first, Garfield and the others at Wizards shrugged off Pokemon as just another weird Japanese craze. But when Pokemon became the first trading card game to outsell Magic in Japan, where Wizards was making $30 million a year, they stiffened their backs. Because Garfield's patent on trading card games didn't apply outside the States, anyone could release such a product abroad without Wizards seeing a penny. But if Nintendo wanted to bring the game to America, it would have to strike a deal with Wizards, or face a possible patent suit. It also helped that Pokemon's young creator, an eccentric video game addict and amateur entomologist, was a big fan of Garfield's. Wizards got the North American rights to publish the game. Pokemon was coming to America.

Pumping a $20 million publicity campaign behind the launch, Nintendo launched the American version of the cartoon show at the end of 1998. With the card game hitting in early 1999, they sent a fleet of lemon yellow Pokemon-painted Volkswagen Beetles to the malls of America and dropped one thousand stuffed Pokemon dolls from an airplane over Topeka, Kansas. When Wizards showed up at a shopping mall to promote the cards, four thousand kids and parents were waiting in line before sunrise.

Seemingly overnight, the cardplaying passion and mania that consumed older Magic-playing teenage boys began infecting legions of prepubescent brainiacs. Kids were blowing so much of their lunch money and study time on Pokemon that schools around the country began confiscating the cards on school property.

Sensational headlines of Pokemon crimes hit the wires. A nine-year-old in Long Island reportedly stabbed another student after arguing over the trading cards. A six-year-old got busted for printing counterfeit Pokemon cards from a Web site and selling them to his unsuspecting schoolmates. "Grownups aren't ready for their little innocents to be so precociously cutthroat," wrote *Time* in a cover story. "Is Pokemon payback for our get-rich-quick era—with our offspring led away like lemmings by Pied Poke-Pipers of greed? Or is there something inherent in childhood that Pokemania simply reflects?"

As usual, controversy sold product. As North American sales of Pokemon cards approached $1 billion, it became clear that Pokemon, like its older brother Magic, was tapping a new world of young cardplayers. While parents were off playing poker or bridge, their small bright children now had a strategic card game of their own.

All around the world, once disenfranchised kids like Finkel—the ones who were a little too smart or too weird to play on the ball fields—now had a means to express themselves and compete from a very young age. Just as kids with musical ability could join the school band or young athletes could join a sports team, kids with brains and strategy skills could develop and discover themselves through Pokemon and Magic.

In the past, there was no such community in place for the future card sharks of the world. They, like Finkel in his early youth, just got lost in the shuffle. Now, however, they had somewhere to go. Trading card games were their Little Leagues, and baseball cards, too. First they played Pokemon. Then, around age twelve, they moved on to Magic. Along the way, they'd meet other gifted smart peers and find a sense of belonging. In pizza parlors, school lunchrooms, hobby shops, they sharpened their minds, refined their skills, and found their edge. And with millions of baby sharks on the rise, there was no telling where they would go.

.   .   .

Every so often, Finkel chalked up another life-altering experience: the first time he read *Ender's Game,* the day he discovered Magic, the weekend he won his first tournament, and, now, with a kaleidoscopic tunnel of lights flashing around him, the night he first tried Ecstasy.

It was a cool October night in London, 1999, hours after the end of a Magic tournament. Finkel had popped the little pill a couple of hours before. A buddy of his from Chicago, a real partier who allegedly had been wrapped up with some drug dealers, talked him into checking out a rave somewhere in the labyrinth of warehouses.

Bobbing there with the flashing lights and Chemical Brothers rocking the rock-steady beat, he felt perfectly in place, connected with other people for the first time ever. Throughout his life, he'd had a hard time connecting with other people, understanding where they came from. And now, in this moment, he felt at one with everyone—even the dancing freak with the propeller hat and face painted like a Lucky Charm marshmallow. Maybe it was just the chemical's artificiality. Or maybe the chemical released something inside him that was real. Either way, it felt really, really good.

Though he was now playing poker three or four times a week at the Diamond Club, Finkel was still plying his trade on the Magic Pro Tour. As the guy who was considered the game's greatest player, he found that his lifestyle choice was having a ripple effect. Magic players, including Pokemon graduates, were now following his lead and storming poker in droves. Money drafting, the Magic games for cash, paved the way. Now word of *Rounders* had spread among the top players, who, like Finkel, latched on to poker's relative ease of play—and potential for payoff. As one Magic player put it in an online forum, "Don't kid yourself—poker is where the money is at."

While the Magic tournament action was taking place at the main tables, Finkel and the other pros were playing poker on the side. They played in coffee shops, in hotel lobbies, in bars, and in hotel rooms. They swapped dog-eared copies of the poker bibles: *Hold 'Em for Advanced Players* by Sklansky and Malmuth and *Winning Low Limit Hold 'Em* by Lee Jones. Suddenly, all the work they'd done for Magic over the years clicked perfectly into focus for poker. Magic players from the Dead Guys to the Jersey Kids had long worked in think tank groups. Now they could meld minds about this new game: Hold 'Em.

Late at night, they sat up swapping tips and tactics: psychology, position, bluffing, the works. Because they were friends, they had nothing to lose, no sense of being proprietary about their tactics. But they knew implicitly that their collective efforts would give them a great edge over ordinary players. Magic was the ultimate farm league for poker. It drew sharp minds, and sharpened them even more. How many poker players have been playing in card tournaments since they were teens?

For most of the Magic players, though, there was one problem with playing poker for money: they were still too young for casinos. Yet, like Finkel, they found ways around this. Certain casinos, such as one in upstate New York called Turning Stone, let players in who were eighteen and over. And when this was too inconvenient, they logged on to the nascent poker sites on the Internet. Finkel's closest friends had discovered poker, too, chief among them David Williams.

After a short stint at Princeton, which he found too snobby, Williams had returned to Texas to enroll at Southern Methodist University and, like Finkel, play poker. At seventeen, he was too young for a casino, but with the help of an older friend he infiltrated Dallas's underground poker clubs. From the moment he walked in, he knew it was a very different scene from what he was accustomed to. "In Magic, everyone's always sitting around joking and laughing," he said, "but this was serious. It was cutthroat." Before long, Williams was among those Magic players swapping poker tips on the Internet.

Like Williams, the more poker Finkel played, the more he hardened. Having reached his full height of six-three, he dropped from a mountainous 250 to a respectable 210. Gone was the geeky baby fat and Kool-Aid-colored hair. In their place was a surprisingly handsome young man who was about to reach a crucial turning point for any aspiring gambler: his twenty-first birthday.

To celebrate, the Magic players took Finkel out for a night on the town during a Pro Tour stop in Amsterdam. They gobbled space-cakes, trolled the red-light district, and checked out the swirling sights. At midnight, they stumbled into an expensive steak restaurant and guzzled the finest wine money could buy. The tourists wondered how these young punks had so much cash to spend. They figured they were drug dealers. No, as one of Finkel's friends explained, they were cardplayers.

Inevitably, they were leaving some people behind. Finkel's oldest and best friend in the game, Steve OMS, couldn't or wouldn't keep up with Finkel's accelerated new pace. Steve's father had had heart problems in recent months, and it had a profound effect on him. Life is short, he realized, and he wanted to make something more of his own. While enrolled at Boston University, he took $85,000 of his Magic winnings and bought a house, which he rented out to some other—older, in fact—college students. He figured he was the only nineteen-year-old landlord in town.

As Finkel descended more deeply into poker playing, Steve watched from afar. "Don't pick up poker," Finkel told him, "it's addictive." Now that Finkel had proved himself in Magic, Steve thought, he was off to another game. But he couldn't relate. His life was on a new track. Just before a Magic tournament in Houston, he phoned Finkel at the last minute to say he had decided to stay in Boston for the weekend. "You know what," he said, "I just want to stay at home, I want to be here for the weekend and see my friends at school. I'm just not going to go." He had nothing left to prove.

But Finkel still had plenty to prove to himself. Though he was long considered the best in Magic's game, and was the sport's biggest money winner, he had yet to capture a big official title—like national or world champion. So one weekend in June 2000, he flew back to the Disney's Wide World of Sports complex in Orlando, Florida, to do just that.

While he was still a relative unknown at the Diamond Club, there was no doubting Finkel's celebrity at a Magic event. Young players queued up to ask Finkel to sign their Magic cards. They hero-worshipped him more than ever. "Hey, Jon!" one said. "You're my idol." The first time Finkel had heard such words, he didn't know what to say. But by now, after hearing this so many times, he had refined his own self-deprecating comeback. "Maybe you should find a better hero," he said, jokingly. "May I suggest Michael Jordan or Bill Gates." Everyone laughed along.

Finkel didn't just act the part of a champion, he looked it. Now down to 185 pounds, he showed up wearing black slacks and a black button-up shirt, neatly groomed. When the television cameras closed in, he stood extra-straight, lowered his ordinarily booming fast volume to a clear slow voice, and represented the game as best he could. He felt as if it was his responsibility. And when the time came to play, he gave the audience the show they expected.

Sitting on the main stage with ESPN2 filming the action, and a microphone recording his every word, Finkel demolished his competition. He cast his Yawgmoth's Will and tapped his Thrashing Wumpus, unleashed his Vampiric Tutor. Players watched in awe as competitors withered in front of what had now been dubbed the "Finkel Fear Factor," or FFF. Even players who had the game locked would inexplicably fold their cards, assuming wrongly that Finkel had them beat.

By the end of the nationals at Disney, Finkel had proved himself once again, crushing his competition to become, once and for all, Magic's U.S. champion. The crowd cheered uproariously. Finkel proudly clutched the oversized check for $25,000 and hoisted his golden trophy high into the air. The photographer from *Sideboard* snapped the cover shot.

As the cameras rolled, the fans and reporters rushed in to congratulate their man. Finkel would now lead the U.S. team to the ultimate Magic competition: the World Championships, held in two months in Brussels, Belgium. Finkel gave interview after interview, posing for photos with his trophy. When a reporter unfamiliar with the game concluded his questions, he asked, "Do you have a nickname, Mr. Finkel, something we can use in the story? I hear they call you Finkeltron."

Finkel winced. He hated the name Finkeltron almost as much as he hated all the other goofy nicknames that had plagued his past: Stinkel, Wrinkle, Tinkle, Ronald McFinkel. But he wasn't a kid anymore. He was a man, a cardplayer, a professional, and if ever there was a time to do something about his moniker, it was today.

Back at the Diamond Club, one of the older guys had given him a more fitting nickname, he thought, one that reflected both his roots and his prowess. Now, in the glare of the spotlight, with the money in hand, Finkel was going to achieve the impossible. He was going to defy the unwritten commandment that a Dude May Not Nickname Himself. This was his game. And people were going to play by his rules. He was going to declare his own nickname, and make it stick.

"If you're going to call me anything," he told the reporter, "call me Jonny Magic."

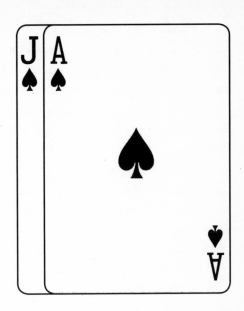

7. JONNY MAGIC

"Oh my God," Finkel realized, as the last track of Pink Floyd's *Dark Side of the Moon* reached its sublime crescendo. "My parents are not assholes!"

It was the summer of 2000. Finkel was lying in his bed in his apartment at Rutgers, imagining the bright planets aligning above him. And it wasn't just because he was frying on acid.

Fresh off his twenty-second birthday, Finkel was finally starting to feel secure. Magic was an international phenomenon with millions of players, and, out of all of them, from Rochester to Russia, Las Vegas to Luxembourg, Finkel was widely considered the best. And with the World Championships in Brussels just a couple of months away, his fans clamored to see if Jonny Magic could become the first Magic player ever to rule both his country and the globe.

But it wasn't just his success in Magic that sent Finkel's head spinning. He was rethinking his relationship with his parents. For years, like a lot of kids, Finkel had moments when he thought his mom and dad were too domineering. They smothered him with their expectations: go to school, get good grades, go to a good college, get a job. He rebelled accordingly—skipping school, flunking out, missing his shot at an Ivy League university, and playing cards for a living.

Now, older, wiser, and stewed in hallucinogens, he had come to realize that his parents weren't to blame. He recognized that he had long been, as he put it, a "teenage jackass." His parents, Mark and Claire, were human beings with flaws, like him, and all they wanted was for their son to have a good life. Yes, they still needled him about getting a "real" job, one that, as his dad put it, contributed something back to the world; they worried that he was throwing his potential away on games. Though he had proven his skill at Magic, they still had trouble swallowing cards as a legitimate way to make a living. It felt too much like gambling to them.

But Jon wasn't a child anymore, they accepted, and they had to let him call his own plays. Since he was still paying his own way through school, they didn't have a lot of leverage in trying to sway him, anyhow. Hopefully, he'd stick it out and finish his undergraduate degree. Though Jon didn't discuss it, he had in fact already resolved to do just that. But he was not about to give up his games. He was a card-player, through and through, and his parents would just have to respect that.

As much as he tried to justify his hobby, however, he knew deep inside that his passion for poker was becoming an addiction. He gambled at the Diamond Club now four or five nights a week. Before long, he was skipping classes at Rutgers to wager during the day as well. Other times, he'd stay up playing until five a.m., then drive back straight to a lecture. It was the same pattern he had demonstrated early with Magic: an unbridled need to keep playing until he proved himself at the game. The difference was, in poker, that ramp-up time cost him. After his first few months, Finkel was $15,000 in the hole.

But with the help of Hollywood Mike, he began slowly turning his game around. He learned that the same essential skill that distinguished him in Magic—his discipline to make quick and accurate decisions based on incomplete information—served him well in poker. To play smart Hold 'Em means folding the vast majority of hands. A good player has to have the patience to wait for the hands worth playing. That's not as easy as it sounds, Mike said. After an hour of waiting, it might get tempting to play a suited Queen 10 when another guy raises under the gun. The pros distinguish themselves by having the maturity to resist temptation. They wait for the good hands, and they know what to do when they get them. More important, they accept the fact that even if they do everything right, they still might lose in the short run, but, in the long term, they'll win.

Finkel distilled the Zen of this message into his marrow. As a kid, after all, he had done all the right things—getting good grades, being honest—and what did he get in return? A golden shower of grief. Yet he never wavered. He just kept plugging away. And now, sure enough, he had found the deep blue end of the long run. His suffering made him the star he was today. Less than six months after he started playing poker, he was up $50,000, including more winnings at Magic.

But, even so, he was far from perfect. And, one night, his confidence got the better of him. When a showboating pro at the Diamond Club got in Finkel's face after a bad hand, Finkel uncharacteristically lost his cool. Lashing out at the man, an Orthodox Jew, he made an offensive joke, one he immediately regretted. But it was too little too late. The man, a club veteran, protested loudly, and Finkel got banned from the Diamond for a month.

With his time off, Finkel set his mind back to the meta-game of self-improvement. Over the past year, he had come to realize that he could master his life in the same way he mastered his games. Though he had hardly become a Don Juan, the Pick Up Guide rules were chipping away at his shyness around women. He applied the 3 Second Rule, approaching girls he found interesting on the fly.

During the day, he started attending his classes again. Finkel pumped his GPA up from the 0.7 of his freshman year to a 3.5. He went to the gym and shed more weight. He accessorized his personality, shopping for new clothes, surfing Napster to download songs by bands he'd missed out on during his extended Bon Jovi phase. But he didn't remain in his bed listening to Led Zeppelin for long before the cards came calling again, more loudly than before. The name of their messenger was Alex Balandin.

Alex was a friend of Hollywood Mike's from the poker club. Finkel liked him from the start. Six years older, he was a slightly heavyset guy with longish dark hair, a neatly trimmed beard, and hip rectangular glasses; he shared Finkel's voracious appetite for both food and games. His favorite food was chicken wings, which he ate by the dozen and Hoovered efficiently off the bone.

Like Finkel, Alex was another of the smart weird boys who find solace in gaming. Born in Russia, he moved with his mother to Connecticut when he was three to avoid anti-Semitism. A brainy outcast, he latched on to games from Dungeons and Dragons to Magic, and, most of all, bridge. He loved bridge's inherent complexity, that no matter how good you became, there was always room for improvement. It was another trait he shared with Jonny Magic: that McLuhanesque notion that the games reveal a person, and that a person can better oneself through games.

And like Finkel, Alex was in the games for the money. In college, Alex's bridge club started playing poker, and inevitably made its way down to Atlantic City. Alex excelled at poker, winning a tidy sum and proportionally losing interest in school until he dropped out with just one semester to go. When a bridge buddy recommended him for a job trading options on Wall Street, Alex found the most lucrative application of his math and probability skills yet. Riding the crest of the dot-com boom, he made enough money to retire at just twenty-seven years old—and turn his attention back to his true love, cards.

During his frequent nights at the Diamond Club, Alex, like Hollywood Mike, became another mentor for Finkel. Just as Finkel had thrived by meeting intellectual peers in Magic—guys like Steve OMS,

David Williams, and the Dead Guys' leader, Dave Price—Alex and Mike became his think tank for poker. Finkel repaid the favor by playing Magic with Alex, but the veteran player could hardly keep up with the national champ. As a mutual friend once told Alex, "When Jon plays a card, it's the most amazing card I've ever seen, but when you play it, it's not that good."

After Finkel got kicked out of the Diamond Club, Alex did his best to boost his young friend's spirits by taking him down to a poker tournament at the Tropicana Casino in Atlantic City. Late one night there, Alex had had enough, but Finkel wanted to keep playing. So Alex reached into his pocket and handed Finkel a stack of purple chips. "Can you cash this out for me when you leave?" he said. "I'm going to go crash."

Finkel looked in his hand. There were nearly $2,000 in chips. "Sure," Finkel said, and Alex walked off. The two hadn't known each other that long and Finkel couldn't help but feel somewhat shocked that Alex would entrust him with so much money. After so many years of getting beaten up and kicked around, Finkel valued trust more than anything else. And if Alex trusted him like this, he figured, the feeling was mutual. They would be great friends.

One night soon after, Finkel found out just how much Alex trusted him. The two were playing Magic in the back of a diner over a plate of chicken wings when Alex abruptly asked for the check. Checking his watch, he said he had to go uptown to meet some friends. They were going to play a game, and he asked if Finkel wanted to come along.

"What is it," Finkel asked, "poker?"

"Bigger," Alex said, sweeping up the Magic cards. "Blackjack!"

Finkel and Alex hopped a cab to the Upper East Side, and Alex told it to stop in front of a fancy high-rise apartment building. Finkel followed him into the elevator to the top floor. He could hear the murmuring of voices as they approached the doorway. Inside the lavish one-bedroom apartment were about a dozen people crowding in small clusters around three card tables covered in green felt. Finkel recognized one of the dealers from the Diamond Club. But this time he was dealing blackjack.

Finkel had only played about an hour of blackjack in his life, but he recalled the rules. Unlike poker and Magic, players don't compete against one another, but against the dealer. The object is to outscore the dealer's hand without going over 21 points. Points are scored according to the numeric value of each card. Face cards are worth 10; an Ace counts for either 1 or 11, depending on the player's choice. Each other card's value corresponds to its number.

At the beginning of the game, each player makes a bet, then is dealt two cards faceup. The dealer deals himself two cards as well—the first facedown, the second, known as the upcard, faceup. If the player or dealer starts out with an Ace and a face or 10 card, that makes 21 or blackjack; players who nail a blackjack are paid at a rate of 3 to 2 on their bet, unless the dealer also has blackjack. When a player/dealer tie happens, it's called a push, which means the player hangs on to his opening bet.

If neither the dealer nor the player has 21 in the opening hand, then the player has four options for what to do next: hit, stand, double-down, or split. To take more cards and try to score closer to 21, a player hits; this is signaled by either tapping or scratching the felt. When not wanting more cards, a player "stands" by waving her hand facedown over the cards. If a player thinks she can reach or get close to 21 with just one card, she can double-down, which means making an additional bet equal to her original one, for which she'll receive one final card. In a case when her initial two cards have the same value, she can request to split them and play each hand separately. A player who exceeds 21 points at any time busts, and loses her bet.

Compared to the player, the dealer behaves like a machine. The last to play, he must continue hitting until he scores at least a 17. If he beats the player's score, the player loses her bet. If he ties, it's a push. If he busts, the player gets paid back at a rate of 1 to 1, and experiences that delicious rush of emotions that only a player can.

But Finkel wasn't an average player. He was a budding professional. And he questioned the value of blackjack for one reason: it seemed too much of a gamble. Though casino-goers enjoy the relatively simple rules and fast action of the game, the odds greatly favor the house. An average player is at around a 2 to 3 percent disadvantage against the dealer, meaning a loss of $10 to $15 for every $500 bet. Finkel made a living off games of skill, after all; he found the winning edge in both Magic and poker, so he wasn't keen on throwing his money down the drain now. He wasn't a gambler. Gamblers are suckers. He was a shark. Blackjack was for fish.

But the longer he watched the games of blackjack unfolding in the apartment around him, the more he started to think there was far from an ordinary game going on. As a baseball-capped guy was being dealt cards, a muscular man in a business suit kept asking, "What's the count? What's the count? What's the count?" In the corner of the room, a large whiteboard had been set up in a corner, scribbled with a calendar of casino names and dates. A tall and hefty middle-aged woman in tight black pants and a black tank top added a few numbers with her Magic Marker.

These people weren't fish, Alex said. They were pros. They worked together to track and play cards so that the mathematical advantage shifted in their favor. They were a card-counting team. And as Alex pitched to Jonny Magic, their newest recruit, they were the best.

Alex, Finkel learned, had been beating the game of blackjack for years. Alex started before he was twenty-one, when his budding interest in gambling led him to the essential books on the subject: *Professional Blackjack* by Stanford Wong, *Million Dollar Blackjack* by Ken Uston, *The World's Greatest Blackjack Book* by Lancelot Humble and Ken Cooper, and, the first of them, *Beat the Dealer*.

In 1962, a University of California math professor named Dr. Edward O. Thorp penned *Beat the Dealer,* which giddily detailed how he employed his coveted IBM 704 computer to devise and execute a winning strategy. "As I picked up my winnings and left [the blackjack table]," he wrote, "I noticed an odd mixture of anger and awe on the dealer's face. It was as though she had peeked for a brief moment through a familiar door into a familiar room and, maybe, she had glimpsed something strange and impossible." The book became a sensation, fueling numerous "Prof Whips Vegas" headlines, and forcing casinos to change their game play. But there was no turning back the tide; the age of card counters had come.

The technique, as it eventually evolved, is based essentially on two main principles: a rule set for optimal play called "basic strategy," and a technique for counting cards. Basic strategy, Alex told Finkel, breaks down how a player should play every possible hand in every possible situation: say, stand on a hard 17 or higher, double-down on a 9 against a dealer showing a 3 through 6, or split 6s against a dealer's 2 through 7. If a player can't brand the rules into his brain, he could always download and print it out on an index card from the Internet. Walk into any casino and there will be someone quadruple-checking the basic strategy card in his sweaty hand.

The more advanced strategy is the count, Alex said. Generally, casinos deal a combination of six to eight decks at a time from a dispenser called a "shoe." In blackjack, a player's odds of winning improve when there's a greater concentration of Aces and 10s remaining in the shoe. This is true for two reasons: it increases the likelihood of hitting blackjack, and the chances that the dealer, who must hit until he reaches at least 17, will bust.

In short, blackjack, unlike other casino games, has a memory. Every card dealt means one less of that rank remains. Thorp calculated that a set of remaining decks containing a greater concentration of 10s and face cards could raise a player's advantage to as high as 5 percent, bringing a $25 earning for every $500 bet; on average, the advantage hovers around 1 to 2 percent—not enormous, but an edge nonetheless. This is considered a "positive" deck. The fewer 10s in the remaining shoe, the worse the odds, the more negative a deck. The trick is keeping track of the 312 cards of the shoe.

Blackjack pros don't literally count every Queen, Jack, or Ace; instead, they assign a simple, corresponding value. One of the more popular solutions is called the Hi-Lo Count, which reduces each card to either a −1, 0, or +1. The so-called 10 cards (10, J, Q, K, A) get a −1 value, the idea being that for every one dealt, there's one less remaining in the deck. Cards 2 through 6 get a +1 count, and cards 7 through 9 are 0.

As the cards are dealt, Alex explained, a player keeps track of the running count, which represents the value of the cards that have been removed from the shoe. When the count gets notably positive, that indicates that there are more 10s and Aces remaining in the deck, thus spiking up the odds for a high hand or blackjack. For greater precision, a so-called true count is determined by dividing the running count by the approximate number of decks remaining.

To succeed as a card counter, one needs both the discipline to keep track of the fast action under the hot lights, and the chops to play perfect basic strategy. Plus, the game requires the constitution to ride out the bad swings. A positive count only comes up around 15 percent of the time, which means lots of waiting—and losing. And even when the count is good, there's still almost a 50/50 chance that the bets will go down the drain. To win in the long run requires a fat enough bankroll to survive the losses and solid enough guts to ride out the swings. In all, life as a card counter is far from easy. But, as in any pursuit, some people just have what it takes.

Alex told Finkel that when he tried out his skills in Atlantic City, he quickly discovered that his card smarts and math chops made him a winner. Over his first year of weekend trips to AC, he was soon betting purple $500 chips and raking in more than $100,000.

"Isn't this illegal?" Finkel asked.

"Can it really be illegal to use your brain?" Alex replied.

While it isn't illegal to count cards, it pisses off casino operators no end. The casino owners built their palaces on their edge, after all, and that's just how they want to keep it. Outside Atlantic City, casinos simply 86 anyone caught counting cards; as privately run facilities, they have this right. In AC, they can't boot card counters, but they can change the game on the fly. Like Magic and poker, blackjack comes with its own meta-game.

In the Thorp years, it certainly wasn't hard to figure out that the nerdy guy with the wrinkled brow and enormous stack of chips was probably counting cards. As a result, counters became notorious for their brief shelf lives. Then they discovered that they could get by much more easily with a little help from their friends. They could do precisely what a generation of Magic players, and countless other wise minds, had done to improve their work. They could share knowledge; cover for each other; develop systems, signals, roles, offensive and defensive strategies. They could form a team.

The large woman swilling coffee by the whiteboard was Sylvia, the cofounder of the team. Beside her stood a muscular, bald guy with a big nose and face; this was her younger brother, Vinny. Alex said he met them through one of his friends on Wall Street. And he was glad he did. Together, he told Finkel, they were making millions.

To some extent, they employed the same strategies pioneered by the earlier card-counting teams. In the mid-1970s, Ken Uston, a senior vice president of the Pacific Stock Exchange, led the first blackjack team to take casinos for millions. Founded by Al Francesco, the owner of a fledgling fried-chicken restaurant, Uston's team worked the casino in a small group with shrewdly defined responsibilities.

One person was a spotter, in charge of keeping the running count at a table. When the count became positive, a person called the controller confirmed the count and would direct the bets to exploit the high probability of good cards remaining in the shoe. The controller then signaled another team member, called a Big Player, to make the bet. Sometimes, to take advantage of the positive count, players also had to deviate from basic strategy.

Noticing a spate of big wins at blackjack in the 1970s, the casinos employed the Griffin Investigations detective agency to bust up the action. Before long, team members would get escorted out of casinos the moment they walked in. To avoid getting thrown out, they started wearing disguises and varying their bets to avoid giving themselves away.

A born swashbuckler, Uston taunted Griffin and embraced the indulgence of the times. He'd streak through casinos, bang hookers regularly, party long into the night. A subject of *60 Minutes* and many other news reports, he even took on the Vegas casinos for trying to boot him out for beating the blackjack game. When Uston died in 1987, the reign of the first card-counting team was done.

Other teams came and went. But in the 1990s, a new and notorious squad was on the scene. Comprised of students from the Massachusetts Institute of Technology, the so-called MIT Team at first kept a considerably lower profile. For a while, they just hunkered down and played, as swiftly and stealthily as possible. But as the money began to flow, some of the roughly twenty-five players, much to the consternation of the others, began treating their work as more of a recreation than a business. In-fighting erupted. Before long, Griffin got wise and, after tracking down the counters' photos in old MIT yearbooks, began beating them at their own game.

By the millennium, the casinos seemed to get back the upper hand—until the team that Alex joined came to town. Unlike the MIT players, the leaders of this group weren't tender college kids. They were something considerably more imposing: corporate attorneys. If Vegas thought a bunch of card-counting geeks from Beantown were tough, wait until they scrapped with a bunch of New York lawyers.

The Lawyers had just started in the past year, Alex told Finkel, when Sylvia and Vinny, both Ivy League–educated attorneys, tired of the corporate grind, quit their jobs and hit the road as a card-counting Bonnie and Clyde. After a few months, they heard that the Rio casino in Vegas was getting bought out by Harrah's. During the transition, the Rio was getting lax in their shuffling at the blackjack tables, making it easier for card counters to exploit the play.

Smelling fresh game, Sylvia and Vinny decided it was time to expand. Through mutual friends, they recruited a team. Some worked on Wall Street, including Alex and a veteran speed skier. And some were among the remaining members of the original MIT team. The Lawyers were open for business. And since the team was run by corporate attorneys, they had no problem developing the one thing the other teams lacked: a solid business plan.

Unlike the MIT group, the Lawyers decided to flip the cat-and-mouse game in just about every possible manner. It was a fittingly cocky New York attitude: we are card counters, hear us roar; we're in the right, it's the casinos who are criminal. Rather than run scared from the casinos, they stood strong behind the law, which was unequivocally on their side.

Drawing on their work experience, they set up their card-counting team under multiple limited-liability corporations. Everything was on the up and up. They paid taxes. They drew up employment contracts. Every new member had to agree to several pages of rules and regulations, from a nondisclosure agreement to a commitment to replace any money that might happen to get misplaced while on the road.

Instead of extending bankrolls over a quarter, they created a new bankroll for each and every trip. They also shunned silent investors. They decided that, after one trip, every member of the team would have the opportunity to invest. But to make sure everyone felt an incentive, there was a rule: players had to physically be on the trip to invest; no silent partners. We're in this as a team. The level of investment was determined by the leaders of the group, based on how long a member had been with the Lawyers, and how much work they did outside the trips. At the end of each trip, the bankroll would be split 60 percent for the investors and 40 percent for the noninvesting players, based on their hours and the roles they played.

The business plan wasn't the only part of the Lawyers that was more aggressive; so was their attitude. Unlike the MIT team, they embraced the fact that, eventually, they'd get caught or "made" at every casino they played. As opposed to playing this eventuality defensively, they got as aggressive as they could without giving themselves away. Because they knew they'd burn their bridge at some point, they understood implicitly that time is money. Since they never knew if they'd be allowed to return to a casino the next day, they took as much money as swiftly as they could.

Though they employed signals and subterfuge, they weren't afraid to simplify their play for the sake of efficiency. They bet round numbers. They used pagers or beepers to signal one another in the casinos. Rather than using a code to communicate a positive count, they would just brazenly bark out the number. And though they sometimes wore disguises, they would hide behind aliases under only a few circumstances. Otherwise, they'd simply be themselves. One time, when a member of the team was asked for identification, he handed over his membership card for the American Bar Association.

Because they knew their mortality as counters—particularly the Big Players who worked the front lines—they employed a dramatically aggressive recruitment policy. Instead of worrying about players getting made, they would recruit a steady and expanding team. If the MIT team had twenty-five players, then the Lawyers would have sixty. They would be the biggest and baddest team yet. Alex told Finkel he thought he had the competency and, more important, the trustworthiness to do for the Lawyers what he had done for Magic and poker. He could be a star, and the rewards could be higher than he ever imagined.

"Next week, for July Fourth, the team's going to Vegas," Alex said. "Why don't you come along?"

Finkel looked around the room. He had been around gamers his entire life, and every new game seemed to reveal a different part of him. In high school, he wandered into Fun and Games in England and discovered his talents for the world of fantasy games. In college, he traveled the Magic circuit and unleashed his raw talent for strategy and competition. With poker, he confirmed his innate ability to make quick, dependable decisions based on incomplete information. It was this skill that enabled him to find the winning edge, to transform what seemed like a game of chance into a game of skill.

As he watched the dealer flicking cards across the table, and the team of players barking out counts, he felt an itch. It wasn't just the game or the money that intrigued him. It was the people. They didn't want to live the life they were supposed to: grow up, go to college, work nine to five, have kids, hit the suburbs. They were sharks, in life and in play.

But Finkel, since getting booted out of the Diamond Club, was finally playing by the rules. He was improving his grades. He was considering a life on Wall Street. Did he want to throw that away to hit the road with a bunch of card counters? Or did he, once and for all, want to live a life outside the games? Finkel knew precisely what answer to give Alex.

"Sure," he said, "book me a ticket."

He was going to Vegas.

Finkel rifled through his papers, cramming for his test. As usual, he had barely studied at all. He snuck a few peeks at the papers in the bathroom and late at night in bed. This time, however, he felt a bit more nervous than usual. There was much at stake in this exam. It wasn't a grade. It was his future with the Lawyers.

It was the week of July 4, 2000, days after Finkel's introduction to the team. He sat on a couch inside the one-bedroom apartment in Henderson, Nevada, that served as the team's headquarters. Two makeshift blackjack tables had been set up in the living room. There was another in the kitchen. The giant whiteboard, listing a dozen casinos and the initials of the team members scheduled to play them, was set up in the bedroom. Sylvia stood before it with her mug of steaming coffee, conferring with her brother, Vinny.

Fifteen members of the team had come out for what was sure to be a busy week. Super Bowl weekend, March Madness, Labor Day, the Final Four, July 4—these were all prime times to hit Vegas because, with all the high rollers in town, it's not as suspicious when the team is making huge bets.

But Finkel wouldn't be doing any betting today. Before he hit the casino, he had to pass his spotter test. While playing perfect basic strategy, he first needed to keep a running count through six decks of cards in under two and a half minutes, making no more than ten mistakes. If he did this accurately ten times, he could move on to the second and more difficult phase: playing perfect strategy while keeping a count over five shoes—each of which contained six decks of cards. Three times during each shoe, he would be asked for a count. Over the course of the 1,560 cards, Finkel was allowed to make five counting mistakes. If he made even one strategy error, the test was over.

Finkel leafed through the papers Alex had printed out for him before their flight. In between his visit to the team apartment in New York and his flight to Vegas, he had gone to a small Magic tournament in Pittsburgh. He managed to look over the material in the car a bit, and here and there otherwise. He wasn't the only one feeling jittery. Beside him on the couch sat the Lawyers' four other new recruits: a young Orthodox Jew in a yarmulke, and three fledgling actors from Los Angeles. Finkel recognized one of the actors; he played the bully who beat up the star kid in a popular sitcom. The other guys played bit parts in the TV show *Touched by an Angel*.

Though Finkel was told their names, he immediately adopted the Lawyers' protocol of referring to everyone by their initials. This was how everyone was listed on the big whiteboard and, for added cover, in the team's elaborate database. As in any other corporation, the Lawyers kept meticulous records of every trip, noting each player's results, hours played, and level of "heat"—the suspicion generated at the casino; the scale ran like Tabasco sauce, from Slight to Medium to Hot to 86'd (when a player was shown the door).

If all went as planned, however, Finkel wouldn't be generating too much heat once he was unleashed. He was training to be a spotter, not a Big Player—who would draw the most attention by making large bets at a table. His job was strictly to be the brain, to keep the count. That's what Alex thought he would be best at doing. The other pledges to the group, the actors, were training for the roles of BPs.

Though he was excited to join the team, Finkel couldn't help letting his assigned role stick in his craw. Spotters got half the pay of Big Players because they were not taking as much risk at generating heat and getting tossed. Finkel wanted his shot at the limelight just like the rest of the guys. But Alex told him his brain was too valuable to waste in that position. Instead, he'd be more effective as a spotter and then, eventually, as a controller—the one who counts and directs the Big Player's plays. It would probably take months for Finkel to pass the more complicated controller test. What Alex didn't tell him was that, despite Finkel's many talents, he didn't think he had the social skills yet, or the tact, to handle the cool act of the big plays.

Finkel nervously chatted up the actors while waiting for his spotter test. Good-looking and energetic, they regaled him with their adventures in Hollywood. After Finkel's prodding, one claimed to have slept with both Tara Reid and Jaime Pressly. Finkel, still something of an Average Frustrated Chump, despite his best efforts at Pick Up Guide techniques, gnashed his teeth.

Finkel sat at the felt and took a deep breath. Vinny shuffled the cards and gave him a nod. Finkel locked on target. As the cards fell across the table, he compartmentalized his brain into two halves. One part played his hand; the other kept the count. This was his skill, his ability to think ahead, just as he had during all those Magic tournaments. In Magic, he had to think about his hand, his opponent's hand, the cards he might draw, and the way his spells and creatures worked together. Right now, he had only two pieces of information to manage—and it felt like a breeze.

As the last card fell, Sylvia sipped her coffee and shot a glance at her brother. "We didn't have any doubt that you'd pass this," she said, turning to the big whiteboard. She wrote the letters JSF in the column next to the Riviera.

It was time for Jonny Magic to hit the Strip.

"The power of Christ compels you! The power of Christ compels you!" the man sang as he danced in the fountain at the Mandalay Bay casino in Las Vegas. He had a rain cap pulled down around his ears, and his baggy khaki pants rolled up to his knees.

A few minutes before, he was placing $25 bets at the blackjack table when all of a sudden he said he needed to anoint himself with holy water. Grabbing his chips, he dashed for the fountain, leaping inside in a moment of delirious rapture, shouting "The power of Christ compels you!" When he then sprinted back to the blackjack table and slapped down a bet for $10,000 and won, no one batted an eye. Even the pit boss could tell that the guy was nuts. They would sooner attribute his win to sheer dumb luck or holy water than suspect that this lunatic was part of a card-counting team. But that's exactly who Gems was, as Finkel learned, the best Big Player on the Lawyers.

Having passed his spotter test, Finkel was heading into the fire. And he was learning the ropes from the best, the guy with the initials GEM, or Gems for short. Big players generated the most heat, because they were the ones placing the bets. And the bets they placed were inherently suspect. Before getting a positive count, they'd play the table minimums, if they were playing at all. When the count went high, they'd be called in to start betting big to take advantage of the high probability of good cards. If handled tactlessly, the wide swing of bets could be a dead giveaway to the casino. Though the Lawyers knew they'd get 86'd eventually, the art of the Big Player was to maximize profits before time ran out. The best way to do this was to create distractions.

Gems, who was dark-skinned, could pass for a variety of ethnicities. Sometimes he'd show up dressed as an Arab sheik. Other times he dressed as a blue-collar Mexican. The rain cap man was his role as a drug-dealing loan shark. As this character, he'd sit at the table and regale the dealers and players with stories of busting the kneecaps of "clients."

His favorite persona was Goldie Baller, a fictional rap artist. Dressed in a tracksuit with a thick gold necklace and fake gold caps on his teeth, Goldie would smash down at the table and start improvising lyrics to songs he made up on the fly. Before long, he'd be sitting there with two gorgeous women by his side. People hardly noticed the suspicious swing of bets he was unleashing at the table.

The distractions helped for another reason. When players win more than $10,000 they have to show ID when they cash out their chips. It's a process known as a Cash Transaction Report, or CTR. Using fake credentials was a serious crime, and the Lawyers would not cross that line. Then again, they didn't want to blow their cover unnecessarily. Part of Gem's genius at BPing was his ability to preserve his identity and still keep the CTR intact. He'd saunter up to the cash window in his hip-hop regalia and hand over his chips. When the clerk asked for his ID, he'd provide his real name, then lean forward all smooth and cool and say, "Tell the pit it's Mr. Goldie Baller."

The cashier would call the pit boss and say, "Sir, I have a Mr. Goldie Baller cashing out here." The pit boss would replay the colorful rapper's songs in his head and chuckle and say, "Yes, he's okay." And Gems would be on his way.

Some Big Players kept their own count and were called counting BPs. Others relied on a controller to call the shots, and they would just lay down the cash. These were the gorilla BPs. Ultimately, a Big Player was only as good as his count. And the count, on this day at the Riviera, started with spotters including JSF, Jon Samuel Finkel.

Though he tried to appear cool, Finkel's heart was racing. This was his first time in Vegas, and even for a noncounter, that's a lot to digest. Driving down the Las Vegas Strip at night in a cab had been like arriving in Epcot at Disney World. He passed the Brooklyn Bridge of the New York–New York casino, the Eiffel Tower at Paris, the gondola boats at the Venetian. The Riviera's cheesy cascade of stardust lights outside burned into his eyes. He walked in and felt his lungs fill with the extra oxygen the casino pumps inside. As in all gambling halls, there were no windows or clocks. It felt like descending into the belly of a pinball machine.

Finkel entered the casino with four other spotters and the BP. They proceeded as planned, spreading around the blackjack tables and staking out their territory. Finkel didn't need any disguises today. He just dressed as he had for the past few months—charcoal gray pants, a black button-up shirt—the same outfit he wore at Magic tournaments. After that fateful moment when his glasses shattered off his head while playing basketball, Finkel had done a good job at making himself over. The Jewfro was tamed into handsome curls. Without the extra poundage around his waist, he appeared less burdened; he walked with greater authority.

Taking a seat at a table, he ordered up a gin and tonic when the miniskirted cocktail waitress sidled up beside him. Though the counters played sober, to stay on top of their game, Finkel didn't want to draw any suspicion by declining a cocktail. A gin and tonic was good, he had been told, because he could take the glass back into the bathroom, dump the booze, and refill it with water. First, he just took a swig and swished it around to get the smell of liquor on his lips.

At this time of night, four in the morning, the distractions were few. This was the graveyard shift, which ran from four a.m. until noon. The two best times to play, Finkel had been told, were this and the swing shift, eight p.m. to four a.m. The fewer players at the table, the better; that way the Big Players on the team would be more likely to get the good cards when they started coming from the shoe.

Finkel had about $3,000 in his pocket, a relatively minor chunk of the Lawyers' $700,000 bankroll for the trip. The table was a $25 minimum, with $1,000 max. But Finkel didn't think of it as money. The chips in front of him were units, pure and simple. That was the best way to detach—otherwise a player ends up sitting there picturing cars and television sets sliding into the dealer's grip every time he loses a hand. This was a game, and it had to be played accordingly.

As the cards fell in front of him, he followed the protocol: playing his hand according to basic strategy, while at the same time keeping a running count in his head. He knew what to do when and if it got positive. The team had developed signals to let one another know about the count. It could be something innocuous, like setting both hands on the table's edge, or running his palm over his head. Finkel waited for the count to give him an opening for a signal, but it didn't come. The shuffle was bad. And time was money; he moved to another table.

Before long, sure enough, the count began to change. He could see it coming, no doubt about it, the true count—the count of the cards divided by the approximate number of decks remaining, added up to a +2. The deck was positive. It was time to get the BP, and fast, because the count could shift back to negative on the fly. This meant one thing: stall.

Finkel had been briefed on different techniques for doing just that. Ask the dealer to make change. In extreme cases, spill your drink. Just don't lose the count. But Finkel couldn't see the BP, and the hand was still under way. Before him, he held a Jack and a 4 for 14. To buy time, he hit, and got an Ace for a soft 15. He hit again, and got another Ace. As his heart began to race, he hit again, only to get one more Ace, bringing his hand to 17. What had just been a positive deck suddenly slammed into reverse with this flurry of Aces.

Now the Big Player had come over, and Finkel couldn't let him sit down. There's nothing more conspicuous than to have a Big Player pull up a chair and then depart one hand later. The Lawyers had code for red alert: say a sentence with a word beginning with the letter N. That meant, go away.

"No," Finkel said, looking at his hand. "Nice! Nasty!" He lost his cool, nerdily repeating the N words more loudly. "Nice! Nice! Nice!" Just to drive the message home, he ignored the rules of perfect basic and hit his hand again.

The dealer narrowed his eyes. Finkel gulped. He just blew it. And he knew it. No one in his right mind hits the hand he just hit. On top of that, he was throwing out N words like someone suffering from a bout of Tourette's. Though Finkel had been assured by the Lawyers that card counting was legal, it didn't feel like there was anything less at stake. This was a game that he had come to win.

"Hitting hard seventeen!" the dealer announced, before peeling off another card. If the pit boss wasn't aware of the suspicious activity, he would be now.

The card came up a 10. Finkel busted.

Sulking away from the table, he couldn't help feeling like a loser. All his old childhood feelings of worthlessness flooded back in. He panicked, just after the count switched, and then babbled like a fool. Just as he was licking his wounds, a casino guy in a suit came up to him. "Excuse me, sir," he said, "but would you mind showing us some identification."

Finkel swallowed again. He knew he looked young, and figured they were suspicious of this kid at the tables. He'd just show him his identification and be on his way. "Okay, I'm going to make a photocopy of this and I'll be right back," the suit said. But it didn't take long for Finkel to find out what happened.

Not long afterward at the Lawyers' apartment, they broke the news. The latest update to the Griffin book, which listed photos of suspected card counters, had come out, and there on the page was Jon Samuel Finkel, playing cards, working his game. Though Finkel was embarrassed to have gotten into the book so quickly, the Lawyers weren't upset. It was par for the course. In a way, it was something of a consummation: Finkel had been made.

But he wasn't ready to cash in for this trip yet. "Alex," he said, "I want to take the controller test."

Alex stared. No one had taken the test and passed it this quickly. It took the last person six months. Being a controller was the most complicated position on the team; the multitasking was out of control: you had to play perfect basic strategy, keep a near-perfect count, signal a Big Player how to bet, or play a deviation. All at the same time. But Finkel wanted to give it a try.

He holed up in the Budget Suites hotel room they'd rented for the team in Henderson. Finkel practiced night and day, studying plays and deviations on flash cards. To succeed, he had to be flawless—both in his count and in his strategy. By the time the test came around, he felt ready.

Back in the apartment, he sat at the felt while Vinny, Sylvia, and Alex crowded the table. Next to Finkel sat Gems, who played the part of the BP. Both of them would be playing two hands, which quadrupled the tasks Finkel had to manage: keep the count, play perfect basic on four hands, signal the BP. His mind raced. The shoe spread out in front of him as the cards came.

The faster they fell, the more distractions there were. A couple of other veterans on the team started barking out random numbers— 5, 18, 2, 7—trying to put pressure on Finkel. At a real table, after all, he'd be dealing with all kinds of action; this was nothing. "Hey, it's almost three-twelve p.m.!" another yelled. "That's six or is it eight in New York right now, or seven?"

Finkel shut it all out of his mind and focused. His cell phone rang. "Aren't you going to get your phone?" one guy said as the cards continued to fall. He was the one calling Finkel, as another way of messing with his game. "Hey, answer it," he said. "It rang six, seven, or eight, nine, or ten times already?"

The numbers and calls streamed through his ears and he let them drift past. He signaled Gems with each hand, telling him when to stand, hit, double, split. Meanwhile he was managing his own two hands. "What's the count?" Sylvia would ask again and again.

Two hours had passed, and Finkel was going strong. Then the test came to an end. Sylvia and Vinny exchanged glances, then burst into huge grins. Alex was clapping his hands. In the history of the team, no one had ever passed a controller test in less than four months of studying. Finkel had just done it in two days.

The coup was enormous. The deal was that when a member passed a controller test, all his previous hours that trip got paid at the controller rate. Finkel just doubled his money. And the timing couldn't have been better. Over two weeks in Vegas, the Lawyers would end up clearing more than half a million dollars. Finkel, who quickly redeemed himself after his first night spotting, had become a rising star.

"You know, you can get more money by recruiting other players," Sylvia told him one night. "Do you know anywhere you can find a bunch of bright guys like you?"

Finkel grinned and said, "I know just the place."

Creature — Wizard

Shadowmage Infiltrator can't be
blocked except by artifact creatures
and/or black creatures.

Whenever Shadowmage Infiltrator
deals combat damage to a player,
you may draw a card.

Illus. Rick Farrell

™ & © 1995–2001 Wizards of the Coast, Inc. 294/350

1/3

8. THE CARD SHARK KIDS

It was a bright August day as the ESPN2 cameras closed in on the
Exposition Center in Brussels, Belgium. Outside the towering gray
building, the sun sparkled on the giant aluminum orbs of the Atom-
ium, a 334-foot-high, 2,400-ton sculpture of a molecule of metal.
Inside the hall, explosions erupted on stage as ghost-faced saxo-
phonists squealed and catsuited dancers shimmied up wintergreen
ribbons. The 2000 Magic: The Gathering World Championships
had begun.

Seven years after the game hit shelves, this was going to be the
grandest event yet. Fueled by the influx of new players from Pokemon, Magic was bigger than ever. Wizards of the Coast was reaping
the rewards, selling to Hasbro, publishers of Monopoly and Scrabble, for $450 million the previous year; Richard Garfield, who stayed

on as a consultant, pocketed $125 million. The trading card game juggernaut he had envisioned at the waterfall nearly a decade ago had exceeded his wildest dreams.

Today, 271 of the world's greatest young cardplayers had come to compete. Though the game was still considered dorky by many outsiders, the players had become increasingly diverse. There were nerds, jocks, blue-haired punks, chain-smoking thirty somethings, former cheerleaders, valedictorians, and debate team champions. On some level, many had one thing in common: a feeling that they never really fit in. Now, instead of living their parents' dreams, they were trading their vanilla futures to travel the world playing cards. And, not surprisingly, some of them pissed off their moms and dads in a big way. As one of the female pros put it, choking back tears, "You'd be amazed at how many of us have been thrown out of our parents' homes."

But all that was behind them today. They lined the long tables under the towering arches of the Expo hall, eagerly ripping fresh Magic cards from their shiny silvery wrappers. Fifty teams from Singapore to Slovakia had come to play for $250,000 in cash prizes and the two big trophies: team and individual champions of the world. In the seven-year history of Magic, no one player had ever walked away with both titles. But as the ESPN2 cameras trailed a tall curly-haired player through the crowd, it was clear when the favorite, Jon Finkel, had arrived.

Since his first Pro Tournament in 1996, Finkel had solidified his standing as the Bobby Fischer of the game. He had become the number one money earner with $151,426 in winnings. He proved to Pokemon and Magic fans around the world, as well as to Garfield and the people at Wizards of the Coast, that, contrary to popular belief, you're never too young to make a living playing cards. When asked on ESPN2 how he felt being the top pick, Finkel answered with authority. "It's easy to be the underdog, because no one expects you to win," he said, "but I prefer being expected to win. It puts pressure on you. If you lose, you're going to let people down."

With each step toward the arena, he was swarmed by Magic players who wanted him to sign their Ophidian—the card renowned as his favorite. As he wielded his pen and posed for photos, he didn't tell any of his admirers his old line that they should consider finding another hero. After years of being the reluctant icon for smart, weird boys around the world, he had begun to accept his role. Knowing that he'd be on camera, he wanted to represent the game as best he could. Gone were the baggy jeans and stained T-shirts; today he wore a shirt and tie.

But the crowds in Brussels had no idea what other kind of cards their boy wonder was playing. Since joining the Lawyers' blackjack team, Finkel had kept his new career quiet. As part of his deal with the team, he signed a confidentiality agreement. The last thing he needed was to be counting cards in Vegas and have a Magic player walk by and shout out his name. His mug was already in the Griffin book, after all; he didn't need to make it easier for the casinos to find him.

While he didn't publicize his blackjack play, however, he did bring it up with a few of his closest friends from the game. And he had good reason—he wanted them to join him. Now that he was an official member of the Lawyers, Finkel had the opportunity to both invest in each trip's bankroll and to increase his stake. For each recruit he brought on to join the team, Finkel would receive an additional one-eighth of a base share, or 12.5 percent.

But he couldn't simply draft anyone off the street. As Alex explained to him, the winning recipe for recruits was "good people with good brains." This meant that they had to have the intellect for counting and strategy, the constitution to ride out the bad swings, and, most important, trustworthiness. Card counting is a cash business—and there is always plenty of cash around. When someone on the team pocketed thirty or forty grand at a blackjack table, the team had to know the player wasn't going to hit the road.

There was one other quality that Alex didn't mention explicitly, but Finkel knew nonetheless: a card counter had to look cool. The biggest giveaway was if someone looked like a mega-nerd. Who else would you expect to have the brains to keep track of hundreds of cards? If a pit boss saw an awkward young white kid furrowing his brow at a table, he had a pretty good idea who to bust. The old Finkeltron wouldn't have stood a chance. The new Jonny Magic was tailor-made.

Considering the third criterion, Finkel knew his pool of recruits was reduced the moment he looked around the Expo hall. Though many Magic players, particularly the pros, sported the default millennial dude getup—backward baseball cap, goatee, indie rock shirt—there were still a fair share of dandruff-dusted brainiacs in high-water slacks. But there was one person who immediately stood out: the Dead Guy himself, Dave Price.

Dave had long built a reputation in the Magic world for both his expert game play and his phenomenal integrity. As one of the leaders of the Dead Guys, the team of student players from Cornell, Price had led the fight against the early generation of cheaters and scoundrels on the burgeoning Pro Tour scene. He had also become one of Finkel's closest friends on the circuit.

Like a lot of the top Magic players, Dave was too independent and stubborn to subscribe to the American Dream of a day job, family, and house in the 'burbs. Though some of their friends had begun working on Wall Street, applying their hustle and numbers skills to trading options, Dave was among the holdouts. He paid his bills with his Magic winnings, and money he made editing a Magic Web site. Finkel knew he was ripe for plucking.

"Look, Dave," he told him, "I'm part of this card-counting team. You don't have to risk anything at first, but believe me you'll want to later on when you can. I think you'll be a good fit."

Dave listened intently to his friend. It hardly shocked him to hear of Finkel's latest exploits. Though Finkel was unknown outside the insular world of Magic and the Diamond Club, anyone who met him at a table considered him among the best cardplayers in the world. It wasn't surprising that Jonny Magic had found a new way to cash in. But when Finkel explained the concept of basic strategy and counting, Dave wasn't sure that he could keep up.

"You can come out to Vegas with us and practice there," Finkel assured him. Dave had to think about it, but Finkel was adamant. "If you don't do this," he said, "you're going to regret it for the rest of your life."

While Dave mulled it over, Finkel went on to more pressing matters: competing at Worlds. Though the U.S. team was the favorite, the finals came down to a heads-up, tiebreaking match between Finkel, the U.S. team captain, and Ryan Fuller, captain of the Canadian team. The two sat under the spotlights at a large table inside a dramatic set of steel girders. At the beginning, Finkel exhibited his usual swagger for the ESPN2 cameras, waving the tiny American flag in the face of his opponent. Midway through, however, Finkel fell silent as he unexpectedly slipped behind.

"I notice you're being quiet now," taunted Fuller.

"I'm just trying to think how I'm going to kill you," Finkel replied, and then proceeded to do just that. The U.S. team took home both the $22,000 prize and the trophy.

With the team title wrapped up, Finkel slugged his way to the individual finals of the event. With this victory, his hat trick of feats—U.S. champ, World team champ, World individual champ—would be complete. But the victory would have to come at a price. Sitting across the table under the lights was his good friend Bob Maher, a former high school jock from Illinois who had become a Magic champ after getting sidelined with a hurt knee. Rather than leave one person short, the two agreed to split the $34,000 first-place and $22,000 second-place prizes. But the trophy would go home with the champ.

To the crowd's surprise, this match, too, came down to the fifth and final game. Maher hit Finkel hard, tapping a combo of lethal cards called the Thran Dynamo and Tangle Wire. Finkel responded by deftly throwing down an Island card and a crippling Voltaic Key. The move blocked Maher's Tangle Wire attack, leaving Finkel to wield his final blow: a brutal card called Colossus. Finkel had successfully whittled Maher's score from 20 to 0 to win the match. As the zebra-striped referee signaled Finkel's victory, the unthinkable had been done. The commentator said, "Finkel is the best in the world, hands down!"

Standing outside on the steps, Finkel clutched the gleaming golden trophy as his necktie flipped in the breeze, posing for the champion photo. When the ESPN2 crew closed in, the gushing reporter said, "The confidence was there the whole time, wasn't it?"

Finkel snapped his gum. "I've got to be confident," he replied, "I'm playing for the Stars and Stripes." He wasn't being ironic. Like a true athlete, he meant it.

He wasn't the only one beaming. Stepping forward from the crowd came Richard Garfield in a blue pinstriped shirt and bow tie under a black vest. His wiry black hair was tousled from the long days of interviews and impromptu card matches with fans. But nothing could take away from this moment. Like a proud father, he reached out his hand to congratulate Finkel on his win.

Finkel smiled widely as Garfield approached. He still was something of a fan-boy in Garfield's presence; after all, this was the guy who invented the game that had such an impact on his life. He couldn't even imagine where he'd be without Magic—probably working a job he hated, slaving away for some boss. He'd always be indebted to Garfield for what he'd done.

The warm regard was mutual. Years ago in graduate school, Garfield had wanted to create a game that would spawn a new kind of mental athlete, someone who could, ultimately, legitimize the world of game playing; now here he was with the person who, by mastering Magic, was making that vision come true. Though Garfield didn't play favorites among his millions of players, he couldn't help having a soft spot for Finkel. He'd seen the boy come of age through his game, transforming from the big awkward kid to the tall cool man. Though he was cautious about taking credit for Finkel's transformation, he appreciated the role he—and his game— played.

"Everyone's teens are tough, particularly when you're a guy like Jon," Garfield later said. "Lots of guys pull out of it. Like me, I went into academics, or others go into stockbrokering. Some people don't need Magic as a tool. But Magic happened to be a tool Jon used to make him feel happy. He might have gotten there anyway, but if Magic was a major part of making his life easier, that's very gratifying."

Garfield and Wizards would soon give Finkel the ultimate honor in Magic: a playing card, designed according to his own rules and bearing his likeness, that would be included in future decks. Finkel named it Shadowmage Infiltrator. The art showed Finkel, dressed as a robed wizard, wielding a staff as he burst forth from a castle in a storm of blue light. Now he had his own card to sign when fans wanted his autograph. It didn't take long for a signed "Finkel," as the card became known, to go to the highest bidders on eBay.

When the World Championship came to an end, Randy Buehler, the veteran player who had become the sport's own Pat Summerall, concluded his play-by-play Webcast by declaring: "Golf has Tiger Woods. Baseball has Babe Ruth. Basketball has Michael Jordan. Magic has Jon Samuel Finkel."

And, as Vegas was about to discover, gambling had Jonny Magic and his new recruits, the card shark kids.

"Okay, player here's got 12. 12! Hit on the 12, 17. This player's got 15. 15! Hit on the 15? Bust at 22. 22! 13! 8! 15! 10! Another 10! Bust 21! What's the count? What's the count? What's the count?"

It was mid-afternoon inside a large, crowded house in a posh suburb outside the Las Vegas Strip, and class was in session again. With their team rapidly expanding in size by 2001, the Lawyers purchased a home to use as a headquarters and a counters boot camp.

There were two blackjack tables in the living room, one in the kitchen, one outside by the pool, one in a walk-in closet. Upstairs, Sylvia swigged from a large coffee cup as she scribbled names and casinos on the big whiteboard. Down the hall was a closet labeled Costumes, which contained getups for Big Players looking to cover their tracks. Rainbow clown wigs and fake Afros piled on a shelf next to a mess of hats—baseball caps, berets, turbans; a collage of magazine headshots, such as one of Arafat, were taped to the door for reference.

Downstairs, Alex was busy testing the new recruit, a young guy with freckles and red hair named Eric Kesselman. "What's the count?" Alex repeated. Eric sighed deeply, and chewed his lower lip. A tall guy in a black silk shirt illustrated with covers of *Playboy* magazine stepped up beside him. A large black cowboy hat hung low over his eyes. "Don't fuck up," he whispered.

Eric looked up. It was Finkel, who had recently become a Big Player, and had taken to this new cowboy persona. Eric offered up a number of the count. Finkel nodded his head. Eric, one of his Magic recruits, was in.

Twenty-two-year-old Finkel was not only the star player on the team, he was the star recruiter—bringing on more new members than anyone else on the team. And his pool of recruitment was Magic. In addition to Dave Price, who joined the team shortly after Worlds, Finkel had soon recruited a team of smart, trustworthy players from the Magic community.

Eric, who had been working as a public defender in New York, was an old buddy from the Neutral Ground days. When he first met Finkel in the early nineties, he, like a lot of players, thought the fat obnoxious kid was a real punk. Finkel at the time insisted on shuffling Eric's deck—something unheard of at the Ground. When Eric asked him to stop bending the cards, Finkel had smiled and proceeded to shuffle them even more violently. While Finkel pursued fame and fortune on the Magic Pro Tour, Eric plugged away at a law career. But as the poker bug infiltrated the Magic scene, Eric got swept up in the craze, and, when Finkel came calling about blackjack, he was ready to gamble full-time.

He wasn't alone. His buddy Ben Murray was another Magic player from Neutral Ground whom Finkel recruited for the Lawyers. Tall and articulate, Murray was a struggling actor in New York who worked Shakespeare festivals and managed a bar at night. Together, Ben and Eric, like their friend Dave Price, had become something of surrogate big brothers for Finkel. Finkel also recruited his friend Igor, a Wall Street trader who had played on the Magic pro scene. And he even signed up his younger sister, Jenny, who was now pursuing a master's in computer science at Stanford. Two Finkels, the Lawyers figured, would be even better than one.

There was one of Finkel's Magic friends, however, who was conspicuously absent from the mix: David Williams. But it wasn't by Finkel's choice. Though he thought Williams had the stealth skills and power brain to make a blackjack king, his old friend had become embroiled in controversy. The incident had happened at a recent Magic tournament. Finkel was money drafting in a corner with some friends when a kid rushed up to him and screeched, "Williams had marked cards! He was just disqualified!"

The judges, Finkel learned, had found three bent Accumulated Knowledge cards in Williams's stack. Williams admitted that the cards appeared marked, but insisted that it was just a matter of wear and tear; knowing where these cards were in his stack would give him no advantage in the game, he argued. But his explanation didn't matter. By violating the rules, knowingly or not, he was disqualified from the event and banned from the Magic Pro Tour for a year.

By the time Finkel tracked him down, Williams was walking around numbly like someone emerging from a car crash. Over the past few years, the two had traveled around the world together, staying up all night, strategizing, splurging on pricey steak dinners. When Finkel first met him, he was sort of like a kid brother, an eager and competitive brainiac looking for his edge. He burned to prove himself even more than Finkel, and would often sink into despair after a loss. Finkel tried over the years to talk Williams out of his funks. Being a card shark meant controlling your emotions, accepting the losses, riding out the bad swings. Though both Finkel and Williams had their share of bad swings, personally and professionally, they dealt with the pain differently. Finkel learned to let it roll; Williams was still mastering that skill. Finkel didn't want to judge him now. He just wanted to support him.

"I'm sorry," he said. "I feel bad."

"I didn't do it," Williams said.

Finkel didn't care; he stood by his friends. Other Magic guys, however, were less understanding. Despite Williams's denials, the controversy was enough to tarnish his reputation among those Magic players who were now risking their money on the blackjack team. Though Finkel would have gladly brought Williams on, he couldn't recruit him under such circumstances. Without Magic or blackjack, Williams chose to set his sights on another game: poker. And Finkel and his crew returned their attention to the casinos.

In total, the Lawyers now had close to a hundred players on the team—dwarfing the previous rulers of the card-counting world, the team from MIT. For Finkel, the ultimate game was on with the ultimate team of players. And now, as he looked around the house at all his friends, he explained the rules.

The casinos lived by taking money from suckers. He had no respect for them. They're dumps, he said, toilets filled with cash. And now they were going to destroy them. "All right," Finkel said, as he lowered his cowboy hat over his eyes, "let's go blow up some toilets."

"Waitress!" barked the lanky curly-haired cowboy in the *Playboy* shirt, as he smashed his chips down on the table. "Get me another bottle of Cristal!"

It was past midnight at the Sahara Casino in Vegas, and Finkel was playing—not just blackjack, but the champagne game. Riding high on their success, the Lawyers had developed a side bet among themselves to see who could have the most bottles of expensive complimentary liquor provided, or "comped," by the casino. Comps are the casinos' way of wooing and rewarding high rollers. These gamblers get so-called ratings cards, which keep track of how much they wager; the higher the rating, the choicer the comps: leather jackets, luxury suites, booze. Dom Perignon and Johnny Walker Blue were tough to score. Cristal was the hardest. But tonight, Finkel was the Cristal king.

Now that he had recruited his friends from Magic, Finkel and his card shark crew relished storming Vegas. For years, the smart weird boys had been the suckers of the world, beaten up, chastised, hung from lockers by their tighty-whitey underwear. On the Magic circuit, they got their first taste of success, but the rewards were limited—the fortune, relatively small; the rock star–style fame, nonexistent. When they applied their brains to Vegas, the tables flipped. They were the winners in a town full of losers, and they were going to cash in.

By now, Finkel had more than just his old posse by his side. He was at the top of his card-counting game. After mastering both spotting and controlling, he finally got his crack at being a Big Player. To do this, he had to not only come out of his shell of shyness—that feeling of being a fat kid from Jersey—he had to shatter it.

He did this partly by following Gem's guidance and developing a kind of meta-version of himself. The cowboy hat and *Playboy* shirt made it easier for him to adopt a swagger. He was Jon Finkel, son of a real estate mogul in New York, and out to spend his fortune. To help lubricate his social skills, he drew on some of the old Pick Up Guide techniques he'd learned online. Just as he had applied the 3 Second Rule to approaching girls, he became gregarious in his dealings with casino staff. The second he felt any heat coming from the pit boss, he'd close in and start talking up the Man.

Inevitably, the pumped-up confidence had a larger effect: Finkel began attracting girls. One night he was on a side trip at Caesar's in Lake Tahoe, Nevada, when he noticed a group of cute college co-eds watching him play. Finkel was in his cowboy hat and had seven racks of chips in front of him. As a counting BP, he was both making the bets and keeping the running count. It required his laser focus.

As the dealer shuffled the deck, one of the girls came up to Finkel. "Hey," she said, "my friends and I are watching you, but we're a bit intimidated. You're probably just a normal guy who's got a lot of money, right?"

Finkel looked at the vivacious redhead with the curving body in tight jeans. Women like that had never approached him in his life. "I don't know if you can really call me normal," he said.

She smiled, and introduced herself as Cindy. As she started up the small talk, however, Finkel had to give his attention back to the game. He was on the team's bankroll, and there were strict rules against violating that trust in an unsupervised environment. But, for once, his focus didn't come easy. She was interested in him, and she was hot. And she was messing up his game. "My friends and I are going to Rum Jungle," she said, stroking his arm. "Want to come?"

Finkel watched the cards fall, keeping the count. "Maybe later," he said, and kept playing. Then he saw her napkin flutter down on the table with her number. He had just inadvertently practiced one of the top rules on the Pick Up Guide site: act like an asshole, and the women will come running.

Finkel wasn't the only one scoring big. As they worked the casinos, the card shark kids, like him, moved to the top of the game. Eric Kesselman became known for his extraordinary runs as a Big Player, winning bet after bet after bet; even with an edge, a card counter can lose money, which is why the team played with such a huge bankroll. But Eric had uncanny luck.

Ben Murray established himself as a BP with a great act, whether it was slurring his way through hands like he was drunk, or playing the role of a character he described as "the Energizer Bunny." Ben would hop around incessantly, clapping his hands like a coke freak and saying "Let's go! Let's go! Let's go!"

Though they couldn't celebrate their wins during a trip, they could unwind on their last night. After a week, they'd divvy up their share of a million bucks and hit the town. This was when they'd flex their comps for all they were worth. One night at the House of Blues, they found a group of hot women at the back of the line, and used their comps to get them all in together as a group to the VIP section. Another night they got a two-story suite with hot tubs on the deck at the MGM, and partied late into the night.

Inevitably, some of the guys would wind up at a strip club. Finkel wasn't a fan of the places; he hated feeling like a sucker. But he could appreciate the irony of his life in those moments. Here he was, the same smart awkward kid inside, but now he was in Vegas with a stripper in his lap who thought he was a high roller. It felt like he was someone else, but it was him nonetheless. To play blackjack, he thought, you need this small little arrogance in you, this self-confidence that you're just a little better than everyone else there. You have money. These people in the casino, they're there to work for you. You don't need their approval. You're the man.

Leaving his friends at the strip club, he made his way back to the casino. By now, he had developed the skill to count not one but two tables at a time. When Sylvia learned of this, she implored him not to tell anyone else on the team. Maybe Finkel could pull off the counting trick, she said, but she didn't want anyone else trying and fucking up. Counting had become second nature, and he executed it with subtlety, turning his back now and then so that it appeared there was no way he could be keeping a count. When the count shifted, he moved in, sitting down at the table and betting big. As he played, a gorgeous blonde in hip-hugger jeans sidled up beside him.

After he was done gambling, he went with her for a drink. This was his last night; the trip was done, which meant he could enjoy himself with his free time. They drank, and smoked, and he told her his story: he was a high roller from New York. And as the words came out of his mouth, he felt that weird dissociation again—he was himself, but not. But then, just as it appeared, the two bubbles collided, spilling together into one identity. It wasn't an act anymore. This was for real.

"I'm going back to shower," she said, putting her hand on his, "but you can come with me if you want."

Finkel said, "Where to?"

"Well," she said, "all my friends are back at my place. Do you have a room?"

"No," he said, "but I can get one." Finkel whipped out his cell phone and dialed the Venetian. Though he had been thrown out of the casino for counting cards, his ratings card was still bursting with points. And, he bet, the casino would be too stupid to connect the dots and keep him from cashing in. "Hey, this is Jon Finkel," he said, rattling off his ratings card number. "I need a room. When?" He felt the blonde's long fingernails running down his spine. "Now!"

As 2001 raced by, Finkel and his card-counting Magic friends grew more accomplished—and brash. On Christmas Day, Finkel showed up at Newark Airport with Eric on their way to Vegas, and the security guard found thousands of dollars in cash bursting from Finkel's ratty backpack. Though Finkel was sporting his ego-boosting cowboy hat, he couldn't mask the fact that he was still just a twenty-three-year-old kid from New Jersey. A cop came over and had one question: How the hell does this kid get all this cash? As Eric stood on the other side of the security gate, Finkel got backroomed.

"Look," Finkel said, "I'll explain to you my situation. I'm a—"

The cop eyeballed him. "If I want you to talk, I'll tell you," he said, as he started unzipping the other pockets of Finkel's bag. He pulled a fat wad of cash from each compartment—$40,000 in total. To make matters more suspect, Finkel's bag was dusted with white powder. Finkel had been taking NoDoz on occasion to get him through the graveyard shifts at the casinos, and apparently some had burst open. The cop ran his finger along the powder and arched his brow. "What's this?" he said.

"It's actually powdered NoDoz," Finkel replied.

"Oh really?" the cop said, snidely.

"Look," Finkel finally said, "I gamble for a living, okay? That's how I got the cash."

But the cop stopped him short, and waved Eric over. "How would you describe what your friend here does for a living?" the cop said.

"He's a professional gambler," Eric replied.

"Where you staying in Vegas?" the cop asked.

"The Four Queens," Finkel said. There was a big game going on at the Four Queens, and he knew there was a room waiting there in his name. "But, hey," Finkel added, "please don't call them up and ask about me. I'm a card counter. I don't want to blow it."

The cop looked at the lanky precocious kid in the big black cowboy hat. Finkel looked like he had stepped out of the pages of *Curious George*. "I'm going to let you go on that plane right now," the cop said, "but I'm going to check into your story. And if anything you said is a lie, you can be sure there's going to be police officers and dogs waiting for you on the other side." He leaned in close. "I'm going to tell you this right now," he said quietly. "Every hundred-dollar bill in this country has trace amounts of cocaine on it. You know what I'm saying?"

Finkel did. Because he was traveling with a bag full of Benjamins, it would be easy for the cop to bust him if he had the inclination.

"But as long as you're on the up-and-up here," the cop concluded, "you're fine."

When Finkel got to Vegas, there were no frothing dogs waiting to bust him. There was just Ben and Igor and Jenny, and the rest of the team. And they had big news: there was a bad shuffle at the Four Queens.

Finkel's blood raced. A bad shuffle, he knew, was gold. At most casinos, dealers shuffle their cards in a random fashion, sometimes using a shuffling machine. But occasionally casinos get sloppy. A dealer instead grabs one chunk of cards from each end and shuffles those together; he'd do this a few times, then start dealing again.

For an advanced card counter, such behavior was an invitation to getting crushed. Finkel, like an elite number of counters, possessed the ability to do something called shuffle tracking. This meant that, in addition to keeping a running count of the cards throughout the entire shoe, he could quantify the count for each chunk of cards along the way. So when the dealer grabbed one chunk from either end, Finkel would know that, for example, the left-hand chunk's count is −4 while the right-hand chunk's is +2; when shuffled together, the new chunk's count, therefore, would be −2. He would do this for each pair of chunks, resulting in an instant count for the entire new shoe.

One of the dead giveaways for a card counter is someone who starts placing large bets midway through the shoe. When shuffle tracking, though, Finkel could come out betting strong at the beginning, which allayed any potential suspicions from the casino. If the high roller was betting big from the start and winning, they figured, it's either luck or magic. And Finkel, the Lawyers knew, was their Magic man.

The plan was hatched. Because of their high heat at the Four Queens from previous trips, the Lawyers would dispatch Finkel in there as the sole Big Player. As a shuffle-tracking counting BP, he wouldn't need any spotters. But he would take along a card eater, a teammate who would bet with him at the table during the negative counts to use up the bad cards along the way.

Back at the house, the Lawyers selected a woman named Angela to eat the cards. Tall and attractive, Angela was the girlfriend of one of the other guys on the team. At one time or another, Finkel knew, she'd pretended to be the girlfriend of just about every guy on the team. She even jokingly called herself "the team whore." But since she was ten years older, Finkel thought it'd be suspicious for a punk like him to be seen with her. They also couldn't be brother and sister, because of their different last names. So Finkel came up with a back story, in case anyone at the casino asked: they were stepsiblings out on the town. Finkel stuffed the pockets of his cargo pants with $30,000 in each pocket, and headed to the Four Queens.

When Finkel's cab pulled onto Fremont Street, the shiny figure of Vegas Vic, the winking neon cowboy who'd become synonymous with the town, seemed to be wishing him good luck. Despite the chill after 9/11, the crowds weren't staying away from the action. Fremont Street bustled with tourists gazing up at the two million light-bulbs flashing in the canopy overhead. Teenage runaway girls rubbed the meaty shoulders of gamblers in padded massage chairs. Flashing signs promised Loose Slots and Prime Rib 24/7.

It was New Year's Eve, and the Four Queens was bumping. The casino looked like a dusty cross between a Wild West brothel and an ice-cream parlor gone bad. Big gaudy swirling light fixtures hung under a mirrored ceiling. Dusty plastic plants poked up from along the wall. Pickled gamblers stumbled over the plumes drawn on the blue carpet. The smell of grime and smoke and liquor breath filled the air. And there, in the center of it all, Finkel eyed the heart of the arena: the circle of tables in the blackjack pit.

Finkel pulled the cowboy hat low over his eyes, and ordered up a gin and tonic at the bar in the back. When the waitress came, he took the drink into the bathroom and swished it around his mouth, then spit it into the sink. Then he webbed his fingers over the glass, and dumped it through. He rubbed the gin-soaked fingers all over his goatee, until he smelled adequately drunk. Then he filled the glass up with water, and stumbled loudly through the crowd to his table. "All right ladies and gentlemen," he said, with purposefully distracting buffoonery. "Happy New Year! Let's play!"

Finkel sat down next to Angela at a table with a $50 minimum and $1,000 max. The dealer, a serious Asian woman, let the cards fly. As Finkel kept the count, he swilled his gin-perfumed water and loudly chatted up the dealer. "Where are you from? . . . How's the casino business these days? . . . Charlotte's your name? . . . That's pretty, one of my favorites." He didn't stop talking for a second. By the time he got through the shoe, he knew the value each chunk had as the dealer shuffled them together.

With the count low, he signaled Angela by rubbing his palm on the top of his head. This meant that she should keep betting at the table minimum, eating up the negative count while he waited for the cards to swing his way. The house was the real buffoon, he thought, and he was in the right. As they kept playing, he simply leaned over and whispered in Angela's ear, telling her how to behave.

After a while, he noticed some of the greasy guys in the pit ogling this young cowboy with his arm over his stepsister's shoulder. Just what kind of kinky relationship did these big spenders have, they wondered. Sensing the erotic subtext at play, Finkel cracked up inside. The art of being a Big Player was to create distractions, and, inadvertently, he had just come up with a winner: what's more distracting than incest?

But despite the good cover and bad shuffle, the count wasn't swinging Finkel's way. In just two hours, he had dropped $25,000. He did his best to play it off—ordering bottles of Cristal to the table, and high-fiving the dealer even when he lost big hands. The moment the count shifted in his favor, his adrenaline surged. He scratched his nose, signaling Angela to get up and leave the table, assuring that he'd get a better share of the good cards. It was time to play.

But there was a problem. Finkel wasn't alone. Sitting before him beside the dealer was a mousy older lady with curly blond hair and thick makeup. Finkel knew he only had a limited period of time with the good cards, and he needed to bet big and fast and score. But this little old lady wouldn't budge, and he watched her score blackjack after blackjack, waving her nicotine-stained fingers in the air. She had to go.

Sylvia had once advised him what to do in such a situation. "Sometimes you have to be an asshole to get someone to leave," she said, "because a sucker's just going to lose some money somewhere else." Finkel looked at the lady, however, and had a tough time mustering the energy. He was still a nice guy inside, and being an asshole still felt like hard work. But when he dropped his fourth $1,000 hand as the lady scored another blackjack, he knew he had to act fast.

"Look," he said to her, "if I give you fifty bucks, will you just leave?"

"Excuse me?" she said.

Finkel pulled a chip from his stack and tossed it in front of her. "There's your fifty. Take it and get out of here."

The woman gasped. "I can't believe you just said that to me," she said. But when she looked up to the pit boss for support, he just shrugged his shoulders. Finkel, he figured, was a sucker, too; just another schmuck losing thousands to the house. There was no way he was going to ask him to leave. Realizing this, the woman gathered her chips and pushed herself away from the table. "The fact that you let this pathetic man play here reflects very badly on you," she said, "very badly indeed."

The dealer rolled her eyes, and peeled Finkel two cards: a King and an Ace. It was time for the magic to begin. As the cards fell and the dealer shuffled, Finkel could do no wrong. In blackjack, dealers cut the cards with a yellow plastic card, putting one chunk to the side and dealing the rest. In ideal conditions, the cut card, as it's called, would be placed approximately 75 percent of the way into the shoe; that way, the counter has enough of the shoe to track before the shuffle. This is called penetration. In even better conditions, the dealer hands the cut card to the counter and lets him slice it in himself. Sure enough, the Four Queens dealer obliged, unknowingly, and Finkel made the perfect cut.

Playing three hands at a time, he soon racked up more than $30,000 after two hours of play. He tracked, cut, bet, playing three $1,000 hands at a time at the top of the shoe. Crowds formed. Players came and went. Two hours later he was up $70,000. Finkel excused himself with another drink, and sped for the bathroom. He spilled his gin and tonic over his fingers, and, looking in the mirror, smoothed the liquor through his goatee. His cargo pants bulged with chips. Looking himself in the eyes, he steadied his mind as his heart pounded. This was not only the biggest score of his card-counting career, it was the biggest of his life.

When he was a kid, Finkel was persecuted for being a smart iconoclast. Now he was getting rewarded for those very same traits—using his brains to score more in one night in Vegas than his peers would make in a year. He hadn't just beaten the game of cards, he felt like he was beating the game of life. And there was nothing that seemed capable of stopping him. Filling the glass with water, he stumbled back to the table—and right into the glare of the casino boss.

They were on to him. Finkel could see the casino chief with his slick hair and his gaudy gold bracelets whispering to the pit boss. After eighteen months as a card counter, Finkel had already been 86'd from casinos dozens of times, and it was no big deal. Some guy in a suit would just tap him on the shoulder and say, "Sir, you're too good for us," then show him the door. But the stakes had never been this high before. The game had changed. He never had so much to lose—and neither had they. So Finkel did the one thing that anyone facing this much heat should do: he met it head on.

"Hey, man!" Finkel called. "Come over here!"

The casino boss darted his eyes at the kid in the cowboy hat and sauntered over. "I'm just here to look around," he said, "see what's going on tonight." Finkel shook his hand heartily. Finkel knew he was the only big action in the house that night, and so did the boss. If the casino suspected he was a card counter, they certainly weren't letting on now. It seemed clear to Finkel that they had him pegged as a sucker on a lucky streak that would eventually run dry. Before the boss left, he comped him dinner for two at Hugo's Cellar, the gourmet restaurant downstairs.

By eleven p.m., one hour before New Year's Eve, Finkel was up $90,000. A crowd had closed in, watching him play. But just as he reached to make another bet, he saw the pit boss signal someone in the back. Finkel could split now, just walk out the door, call it a night. But he was with the Lawyers. They didn't split when they felt the heat like the MIT crew; they made like Icarus flying right into the sun.

Out in the back, he saw a guy in a suit approach him, carrying a steel case. Angela looked over to Finkel, awaiting some kind of signal, but none came. The guy set the case on the table and unlocked the hinges one at a time. Inside were rows of bright orange chips. "In the fourteen years I've been here," he said, "we've never broken out these $1,000 chips. But tonight's the night."

He took them out and stacked them in front of Finkel, row by row by glorious row. Finkel had accumulated so many chips that the casino decided it was time to consolidate, or "color up," his small money into higher denominations. The Four Queens had only a hundred of the $1,000 orange chips, and Jonny Magic was taking every last one of them. With the hour of New Year's approaching, Finkel wanted to get back to the house with the cash before downtown turned into even more of a madhouse.

"Hey," Finkel said, throwing his arm around Angela, "Dad told us to meet him at the Golden Nugget before midnight."

Ordinarily, a high roller, even someone winning chump change, would tip the dealer after a good run. Some people consider it good luck, others just think it is the right thing to do. The Lawyers had another philosophy. Dealers are there to take your money. We have no interest in subsidizing casino staff by tipping them. When we lose thirty grand, they're not tipping us the next day. When we win, should our $500 go to the dealer or a new player on the team?

Finkel had no doubt about it: he was sharing the booty exclusively with the card shark kids. Taking his orange chips to the cage, he cashed out. As he walked out the door, he and Angela stood in the blinking lights of the Golden Nugget as the chorus of "Auld Lang Syne" filled the streets. Across the way, they saw two security guards from the Four Queens staring at them. Finkel nudged Angela, and joked, "Let's go find Dad."

Days later when his flight landed back in New Jersey after the $90,000 night, Finkel almost didn't notice the red-haired cop walking quickly his way. Finkel recognized him—he was the guy from the beginning of the trip, the one with the NoDoz. And he had a very stern look on his face.

"Hey, sir," the cop said, "one second."

Finkel kept walking as if he didn't hear him, but the cop increased his pace. "Sir, sir!" the cop called, and this time there was no going any farther. Finkel stood in his tracks and waited for whatever was to come.

After all these years as a gamer, Finkel had come to see life as a pendulum of swings, dictated by and subject to statistics. Losses begat wins, wins, losses. Every run had its end. Even though he was in the legal right, maybe something had finally gone wrong. Maybe the rubber band of fate was finally snapping back. Maybe the game was done.

The cop patted him on the shoulder. He had checked out Finkel as he said, and it was true. He wasn't a criminal. He was a professional gambler. He could come through airports with bags of cash whenever he wanted, but the cop didn't recommend it. "Next time," he said, "try wiring the money instead."

Finkel laughed it off. The coast was clear for now. But on the other side of the world, a storm was gathering to beat him.

Voidmage Prodigy

Creature — Wizard

◊◊, Sacrifice a Wizard: Counter target spell.

Morph ◊ (You may play this face down as a 2/2 creature for ③. Turn it face up any time for its morph cost.)

Illus: Scott M. Fischer

2/1

9. SEND IN THE CLOWNS

Long after midnight inside the bowels of a government building in Cologne, Germany, Kai Budde sat alone in the dark, waiting for the phone to ring. A hulking young man with a wide shiny forehead and narrow gaze, Budde was fulfilling his civil service duties, answering a senior citizens help line on the graveyard shift. With few, if any, calls coming through, it was a boring job that could lull any other harried college student to sleep in minutes. But Budde was no ordinary human.

On the Magic Pro Tour, where he was systematically crushing his competition, fearful young men had begun referring to him as the German Juggernaut. Ruthless, aggressive, and precise, Budde had been winning more tournaments and money than anyone since a certain fat kid from Fanwood hit the scene. Now he hunched over the computer, spending every spare moment improving his game. There was just one person left in his path, and it was time to squash him.

Across the Magic community, there was talk that the Juggernaut might actually succeed. Since winning both the U.S. National and World Championships in the summer of 2000, Finkel's mind seemed elsewhere. Though he continued to show up at all the Pro Tour events, his wins were winding down. Of course, his closest friends, like David Williams and Steve OMS, knew the reason: he was too busy playing blackjack to keep up with Magic's ever-changing game. But since the vast majority of players, and fans, were out of the loop, they could draw only one sad conclusion: Jonny Magic was losing his edge.

As Budde built his reputation, Finkel's fans struggled to cling to their old hero. Randy Buehler, Finkel's former rival who now worked for Wizards in research and development and as the tournaments' play-by-play commentator, refused to concede Finkel's reign to the Juggernaut. Even after Budde came from nowhere to win three Magic tournaments in a row, Buehler held firm. "If I had to pick one player to win a match with my life on the line," he insisted, "I'd still pick Jon Finkel."

Then Budde won another tournament, and Buehler fielded the inevitable question again: "When are you going to say Kai is the best player?"

Buehler sighed deeply. "I suppose if he wins one more tournament," he replied, "I'll have to give it to him."

Buehler wasn't the only one holding out for Jonny Magic. Another Magic player vowed that if the German Juggernaut won one more Pro Tour, he would eat his hat. Sure enough, Budde thundered to that next event, held in New Orleans, and swept up an unprecedented fourth Pro Tour title in a single calendar year. True to his word, the player cracked open a bottle of ketchup and, banging his fist on the table as his eyes watered, dutifully gulped down his gray fedora. Buehler at last caved in. "All right," he announced, "hats off to you, Kai."

With pictures of the hat-eating episode flying across the Net and word of Buehler's concession making the rounds, the conclusion was foregone. "Before . . . the specter of Jon Finkel and his dominance hung over everything," read one report on the Wizards site, "but Kai Budde is now officially the best player in Magic's history."

Though Finkel, who was approaching $300,000 in lifetime Magic winnings, shrugged off the wallop of the German Juggernaut, his friends suspected he was feeling the sting. Late one night in the Lawyers' house after a long run in Vegas, Finkel and the guys were unwinding over a game of Magic. When the subject of Kai's wins came up, Finkel attempted to rationalize his position. "I could be better than Kai," he said. "All I have to do is work at it. And since I could be the best if I wanted to, there's no reason to work at it."

But that didn't keep him off the Pro Tour circuit. Despite his heading for a six-figure year as a card counter, Finkel attended every Magic event. His friends suspected the reason for his return. "He's going back because of Kai," Eric said.

One cold January weekend in Chicago, Finkel finally had a chance to meet his nemesis head-on. Jonny Magic sauntered in past the autograph hounds looking like a far cry from the old Finkeltron. His hair and goatee were neatly trimmed, and he wore a handsome brown sweater. At his side was Dave Price, wearing a navy blue T-shirt and his hair Vegas-style, in Elvis waves and sideburns. When the two faced off against each other in an opening round, they cracked inside jokes about their blackjack days.

"I'm shuffling Jon Finkel's deck," Price announced. "I don't trust this guy!"

"I'm shuffling your deck, too," Finkel replied. "I don't trust you."

Within hours, to the crowd's delight, Finkel was on the rise—winning his first four matches decisively. The Magic writers hit their computers, banging out word of a comeback. "It's still a bit early to tell," frothed one reporter, "but the Finkel of old may be back."

By the third day of the tournament, their wishes were granted. Finkel had made the top eight and, not surprisingly, so had Budde. When the two players were randomly assigned to play each other in the semifinals, it was too good to be true: the clash of the titans had finally come.

Wizards workers in zebra-striped referee outfits scrambled to set up the card tables onstage. Magic fans climbed the scaffolding for the best view. Cameras trained down, broadcasting the scene on a wall of television screens. Reporters rushed the seats and slipped on their headphones to hear the commentators. Once again, they reiterated that Finkel's decline in status was more a matter of inattention than loss of skill. "Sometimes Jon doesn't care at all about Magic," one commentator said, "but you know he cares about this."

But Budde wouldn't go without a fight. "He's going to try to restore world order against this American uprising," the other announcer replied.

Though just about a year older than Finkel, Budde, dressed in a red ribbed sweater with a dark blue collared shirt poking out, squeezed into his chair like an oversized giant. Finkel sat opposite, hoping the game would be done in time for him to see the Eagles play the Buccaneers in the NFL championship game. "They'd better hurry up," Budde offered. "We're going to miss the game."

"I know," Finkel replied, stiffly, "Go Eagles!"

Out in the crowd, a gangly fan of Finkel's instigated a chant of "USA! USA!" and it was time for the match to begin. Three out of five would win. As the crowd's chant subsided, Budde riffled through his cards and attacked Finkel with a Skirk Commando. But the old pro didn't flinch, coolly peeling a retaliatory Commando Raid from his deck. Budde winced. "You're the master," he said. "This is going to be bad."

It was. Finkel swiftly defended and attacked against Budde's most studied moves, answering his Searing Flesh with a Menacing Ogre, and taking home the first win. As the second game began, Finkel shocked the crowd, and the Juggernaut, by attacking with none other than Voidmage Prodigy, the Magic card that Wizards had designed in Budde's likeness. The card showed a grimacing Budde dressed in armor and unleashing an amoebic plasma blast from his paws. Seeing the card, Budde flinched at the audacity of Finkel's play. The crowd resumed a wild chant of "USA! USA!"

Finkel 1, Budde 0.

"You are so dead!" Budde growled to his rival. The Juggernaut's display of respect was over. Aiming a Cabal Slaver and Shepherd of Rot, he climbed back to take the second game, and didn't look back. Finkel's intuitive moves began to look feeble against Budde's Teutonic preparation. Nothing Finkel pulled could overwhelm Budde's blitz of Festering Goblins and Spined Thrashers. By the fourth game, Finkel was down 2 to 1, and the crowd had fallen into silence.

With his life score near zero from Budde's Nantuko Husk, Finkel untapped his Slipstream Eel. The Juggernaut froze. Finkel stared him down, conjuring the forces of intimidation that Magic players had long ago termed the Finkel Fear Factor. Budde sniffled, and the light reflected on his shiny face. As the Juggernaut peeled off his cards, Finkel's mind assimilated all the information in a nanosecond: the cards, the decks, the odds, and moves. But before Budde could peel off another move, he just thrust out his hand to the German and conceded. Finkel knew he was about to lose anyway, so there was no point in delaying the inevitable. The crowd gasped. The game was over.

The headlines flew across the Net: "Magic King Loses His Crown." Finkeltron might have broken down and cried in a moment like this, just as he did in that first Magic tournament long ago, but Jonny Magic knew better. He had come of age through these games, grown from a geek to a champ, a boy to a man. He knew that you win some, and you lose some. But that knowledge comes at a price. As he left the Juggernaut in the spotlight, he wasn't high or low, he was just steady—a rock, as poker players said. Rocks don't feel.

Mark Finkel sat on his living room sofa in Galloway, New Jersey, on Father's Day 2003 with his elderly dad, Leon, by his side. But his own son, Jon, was nowhere in sight. Since he had learned that Jon had joined a card-counting team, he worried about him more than ever.

He pictured his son, broken and bleeding in some Las Vegas alleyway, the victim of angry casino owners, mob bosses, and crooks.

It seemed like yesterday that he was reading *Lord of the Rings* to the boy late at night in Fanwood. The way Jon took to fantasy and math, the way he spit out binary codes like a human computer, how he argued so passionately about things he couldn't possibly understand—Mark had always hoped he would have been a successful attorney by now. He wished his son was using his talent to contribute something back to society; he always thought Jon, with his analytical skills and big heart, would make a great environmental lawyer.

What would have been so hard about that? Mark, after all, had been much like his son as a young man: a math whiz, an expert card-player. But he didn't pursue a life in the underworld. He got a job. He had a wife and kids. He played the game. Sure, he was now divorced and living in a modest home near the shore, but at least he played by the rules.

But times had changed. Math whizzes like him had become glamour commodities since the dot-com boom. They weren't nerds anymore, they were geeks—fashionable brainiacs. Gone were the days when nerds assumed a life in the trenches of academia or computing. Now they could use their brains not to contribute, but to cash in. The last time Mark expressed doubt that Jon could be making a living at cards, his son showed him a brown paper bag filled with $40,000 cash.

With that kind of money to be had, Mark worried about losing his daughter, Jenny, to Vegas, too. At least she had continued with her higher education, graduating from Columbia to pursue a master's in computer science at Stanford. But now, as he knew, even she was caught up in the cockamamie card-counting scheme. Although he was heartened that she was using her winnings to pay her way through Stanford, he couldn't help feeling concerned. Maybe she was also out in an alleyway, bleeding, he imagined, as he sat on the couch wringing his hands.

Just then, a pair of headlights swept through his window with the purr of an engine outside. The doorbell rang. Mark opened it to find a dapper gray-haired man in a black suit, standing in front of a stretch limousine. "Mr. Finkel," the driver said, "can I help you with your bags?"

Mark took his elderly father's arm and followed the driver into the long black limo. Jon had told him that he was sending someone to drive him to Atlantic City for a special Father's Day celebration. But he certainly didn't want his son to be blowing all his money on a fancy car. When he pulled into Caesar's two hours later, and met Jon standing under the lights, he learned that his son hadn't dropped a penny on the ride. The limo, hotel, and VIP tickets to see his favorite band, Chicago, were comped. He couldn't hold on to the little boy in his mind anymore; his son had become a Big Player.

While this was certainly true, Jon secretly knew that another reality was starting to take shape. Back in Vegas, the Lawyers' tightly run ship had sprung a leak: someone inside the organization was selling information on the team. The Lawyers, it seemed, were in danger of becoming victims of their own success.

Part of their strategy from the beginning was to counter their heat by continually recruiting a new crop of Big Players. When one crew burned out from too much heat at the casinos, another group was brought in. Finkel's team of Magic players had been among the first legion, but now they were moving on to more sophisticated tasks of shuffle-tracking and controlling. In their place came a steady supply of replacements from all walks of life: a fireman, a massage therapist, a New York City cop, even one of Finkel's professors from Rutgers. With nearly a hundred players now on the team, it was getting impossible to keep track of, let alone vouch for, every person who came through the door.

Among the Big Players were Dan and Don, two cheesy older guys from California who seemed to have walked right out of a bad casino movie. With slicked-back hair, big teeth, and open shirts, they regaled the group with their shuffling tricks and sordid stories. Recruited more for their flamboyant personalities than their math skills, the duo did a good job at the tables. But, as it turned out, one of them was up to tricks of his own.

One day at the Lawyers' house, Sylvia got a phone call from an informant friend at one of the casinos. Though the casinos relied on their staffs to bust card counters, the reality was that many of them were enamored of the team's feats. The Lawyers had their share of friends behind the tables. One of these informants broke the news to Sylvia: Don was selling information on the team.

The potential fallout was awesome. On any given night, the Lawyers, who were now pulling in several million a year, might have hundreds of thousands of dollars, cash, sitting in the house. If Don was selling information to casinos, who knows who else he was informing. He could have given the team's address to the mob, for all they knew. The last thing they wanted was for the door to bust down in the middle of the night with a bunch of masked men and machine guns. There was only one option until things cooled down: scram, fast.

But they still had a business to run. Rather than leave town, they stuffed $1 million into a big black duffel bag and rented a cheap hotel room at a Best Western outside the Strip. They would select a dependable person on the team to guard it while the rest of the Lawyers played the casinos. Since Finkel was too valuable a player to keep cooped up inside, they went with the next most trusted person on the squad: the Dead Guy, Dave Price.

Up to this point, Dave, like the other Magic players recruited by Finkel, had embraced the card-counting lifestyle. Making six figures a year, he enjoyed hanging with his old friends, playing Magic on the road, and taking the casinos for everything they were worth. It wasn't always easy; there were bad swings, like the so-called March Massacre, a trip in which the team dropped $350,000. But the upswing always came around if they played long enough. Like Finkel, Dave relished applying his strategic and card skills to a game with much higher stakes. But in the flood of excitement, he had underestimated how high the stakes might become.

Long before the informant sold out the team, Dave and the other Magic players had unexpectedly rough encounters with casino personnel. One night in Tunica, Mississippi, Finkel's sister, Jenny, had a gun pulled on her by an overzealous security guard after she got the boot from a casino. Dave had his own horror show at a trendy casino on the Strip.

After getting caught counting, he refused to accompany the security guard to the back room. He knew his rights from the many lawyers among the Lawyers: you don't have to give your ID to anyone, you don't have to go to a back room. The only legal right of the casino is to throw out the people they don't want playing there. But when Dave made for the door, the big security guard twisted his arm behind his back with a snap and led him to the back. Once in the room, he thrust Dave up against the wall and emptied his wallet for his ID.

The boss then came in and said to the security guard, "You asked him to leave and he refused to leave, right?"

"No fucking way!" Dave screamed. "That's not what happened."

He knew exactly what they were doing: they were trying to arrest him for trespassing, one of the few ways they could legally throw the book at him. But after a brief and intimidating standoff, they let him go on his way. The message from the night—and his bruised and throbbing arm—was clear: don't fuck with us, or we'll find a way to fuck with you.

When the Lawyers came to him and asked him to spend a week in a shitty hotel room with a bag holding $1 million, Dave was less than thrilled. Out of loyalty to the team and his recruiter, Finkel, he couldn't say no. The next thing he knew, he was sitting in the hotel guarding the booty. But he wasn't alone. For backup, the team sent Stew, a former speed skier who had been one of the first recruits on the Lawyers. Day and night, Dave and Stew sat in the room with the money, watching bad movies on cable TV and ordering in Domino's pizza, which they paid for, naturally, with cash. When the maid came, they would take turns sitting in the lobby with the bag until she was done.

Throughout the day and night, team members would come to the room on their way to or back from the casinos to contribute to or withdraw from the bankroll. Every time this happened, Dave and

Stew had to perform the same ritual: dumping the cash on the bed, and slowly counting through tens of thousands of dollars.

As the long days in the hotel room passed, Dave grew weary and anxious. Though the Magic players were known for their steady resolve, their seasoned ability to stay off tilt, the pressure was getting to him. All this money. All this time. And still the specter of shadowy Vegas figures sniffing out their cash. His imagination ran wild. Late one night, as his smudged fingers counted through another stack of Benjamins, he realized he wasn't the only one whose mind reeled. Out of the blue, Stew stopped counting and looked up at him silently.

"What?" Dave said.

"You know," Stew said, slowly, "this kind of money can really change a person's life."

"Yeah," Dave replied, "even a fraction can change someone's life."

Then there was silence. Dave swallowed, as an icy wave of fear passed through his veins. Was Stew making some kind of proposition that they should take the money and split? Maybe this was some kind of test, he thought.

Or maybe it was a threat.

Finkel stared at himself in the mirror for a long time and struggled to recognize himself. Gone was the flabby New Jersey loser with the bleach-blond Jewfro and the baggy stained pants. In his place was a skinny punk rocker. His beard had grown out into an unruly snarl. Yellow-tinted sunglasses covered his bloodshot eyes. A silver hoop pierced his nose, and he had one in each of his ears. Thick black leather bracelets with sharp metal spikes circled his wrists. A pair of handcuffs hung from his ratty black jeans, which frayed over his black Doc Marten boots. He pulled on a black T-shirt with a white skull and the band name "Misfits" scrawled across his chest.

The makeover wasn't for fun. With the heat burning up as he played bigger and bigger at the casinos, Finkel needed a change of appearance to throw the pit bosses off his trail. Packing up his old cowboy outfit, he tried dressing up as a Wall Street executive—

straightening his hair and donning an expensive suit; it was like a glimpse of the straight life he might have led had he not pursued a life of cards. Before long, he ditched the natty threads and suited up as a punk rocker. He had another reason to formulate this new persona: after a long and profitable run with the Lawyers, he was leaving the team.

The decision wasn't completely his idea. After the informant leaked details on the Lawyers, the team's management decided to shuffle its own deck. The team was too big and scattershot, they thought, so it was time to jettison the deadwood and rebuild the squad. But there was no question about who was going to be invited back. The young Magic players had proven themselves to be the most valuable card sharks on the team. Ben and Finkel were now both controlling and shuffle-tracking. Eric was mastering being a Big Player. And Dave, after his long week in the hotel room, had proven his loyalty.

Finkel was ready to rejoin when he learned that his Magic crew had other intentions. They were good enough now to play on their own, and they knew it. More important, they were tired of paying extra and, they thought, unreasonable percentages to the team's upper management. They wanted to form their own team, and they hoped that Finkel would come with them.

Finkel felt torn. At first, he tried to be up front about it and work out some kind of deal where he could play both sides. But the Lawyers, livid at the "clowns," as Sylvia derisively called them, who wanted to leave, wouldn't budge. It was us or them, they said.

Fine, Finkel decided, then he would choose the Magic guys after all. And they knew exactly what name they were going to take for their new card-counting team. The Clowns were coming to town.

Burned out from the heat in Vegas, the Clowns' first move was to take their act on the road. Though they didn't have the bankroll and organization of the Lawyers, the Clowns were good friends with a simple plan: invest what you could afford and split the proceeds as equal partners, Alex, Ben, Eric, Dave, and Finkel, Magic guys through and through.

From the start, the old Magic touch was coming their way. They'd blow into a small town in Iowa or Missouri, and take the riverboat and Indian casinos for all they were worth. At night, they'd pile into their cheap rental car and head back to the hotel for some all-night sessions of Magic. It felt like the old Pro Tour days, traveling and playing on the road.

One day, word began spreading on the Internet about what one site termed "Biloxi's BJ Bonanza." The Imperial Palace casino in Biloxi, Mississippi, was going to be offering a special, paying 2 to 1 instead of the standard 3 to 2 odds for every two-card blackjack, or "natural," a player scored. As the card sharks well knew, this sweet deal added an automatic 2.25 percent to their edge when counting, and an additional 1.9 percent when simply playing basic strategy alone. It was a gold-mine proposition, and the Clowns were on their way.

When they arrived at the casino that afternoon, however, they realized they weren't alone. Though the special was not scheduled to begin until midnight, the tables were already full. The Clowns knew exactly what they were full of: card counters. They had never seen anything like it. An entire casino full of blackjack teams. They recognized faces from the MIT team, Big Players who had passed through the Lawyers, dozens of players in baseball caps and sunglasses and fake wigs, staking out their territory for when the clock struck midnight.

The Clowns jockeyed for the last available seats, and, like everyone else, played basic strategy making minimum $5 bets for the next several hours. Card counters remained glued to their chairs, swearing off even bathroom breaks for fear of giving up what was sure to be one of the most profitable seats in years; if they had had some adult diapers, they would have considered putting them to use.

Sure enough, when the clock struck midnight, every single card counter in the house switched from the minimum bet to playing $1,000 hands. It was so absurd, the Clowns just had to laugh as the purple chips fell their way. It didn't take long for the casino staff to realize they'd been made. But the staff was committed to its special offer and didn't want to alienate the local dads who had saved up their paychecks for this special day.

Instead, they began to slowly back off the promotion. After an hour, they lowered the table maximums to $500. A bit later, they backed it down to $300. Soon they restricted players from playing more than one hand at a time. By eight a.m., every single blackjack table in the house had been shut down except for one table in the middle. But it was too little too late. The Clowns blew out of Biloxi with $30,000 in the bag and huge smiles on their faces.

To celebrate, they decided to cash in some of their long-accumulated comps at a casino in New Orleans. Though they had been banned from playing there long ago, nothing was stopping them from getting a few free nights in the suites. When they called, however, the operator told them she couldn't look up their information because her computers were down. Dollar signs flashed before their eyes. With the computers down, the Clowns had free rein to count at the casino, which had a notoriously bad shuffle, without fear of getting backed off. Flooring it to New Orleans, they took down the casino with a vengeance, bringing up their winnings to more than $100,000.

But, as Finkel well knew, the Bible Belt casinos played by their own rules, too. He learned this the hard way in Shreveport. Finkel had spent a long night playing up his punk rock getup, which seemed even more sensational in such a small town. A trashy older waitress leaned down and cooed, "What are your handcuffs for?" Finkel, at the top of his game, replied, "Why don't you come back when you get off work and find out."

It was just like the Pick Up Guide had said: he never looked like more of a jerk in his life, yet he seemed to be a chick magnet. A bit later, a woman sat beside him and ran her hand up his leg. "Hey," she said, lashing her tongue in his ear, "you got any toot? I got some back in my car if you want to come back and smoke it."

"No thanks," he said. "I don't really go for that stuff anymore."

The sleaze in the town was palpable, and it was only getting thicker. On his way out the door, he was stopped by a huge security guard. "Can we see some identification?" he said.

Finkel, knowing his rights, hit the reply button in his brain. "No," he said. "I think I'm going to leave anyway, I was on my way out."

"Okay," the goon replied, taking him by the arm, "we'll lead you out." But they weren't heading for the door. They were heading for the back room.

"No," Finkel said, shaking them free. "I'm not going to go that way, I'm going to take the stairs." But as he quickened his pace, they walked faster after him. By now, Finkel had lost his teammates. He had no ride, nowhere to go. Finkel saw a taxi line outside and started waving them down.

The goon called after him, "If I ever see your face around here again, I'm going to break it, white boy!"

Finkel stopped in his tracks. *Did that guy just call me "white boy"?* The security guard was white himself. What an idiot, Finkel thought, and something inside of him snapped. All his life he'd been chased by goons for doing nothing more than using his brain. He had it. "I bet you feel like a really big man now," he said, turning back.

The goon stiffened. "I called the police on you," he said.

"Fine!" Finkel replied, knowing he was in the legal right. "Bring 'em on!"

Two cops came and led Finkel around a corner. When Finkel went to remove his leather jacket, the cop grabbed his gun and said, "Hold it right there!"

Finkel put his hands up, shaking his head.

"We don't think he's twenty-one, Officer," the goon explained. "And he won't show his ID."

"Look, sir," Finkel said, "can I have a word with you a minute?" The cop waved him over. "Officer," Finkel said, quietly, "I'm a professional card counter. I know they know it. My name is valuable to me. I'm perfectly willing to show you my identification to prove to you that I'm over twenty-one years old, but I don't want them to see it. I don't want them to have that information."

The cop took his license. "I'm going to see if you have any warrants out for your arrest," he said. Finkel puffed. It was bullshit. He was perfectly legal, smart as ever, and now they were treating him like a criminal. Finally the cop came back. "All right, Mr. Finkel," he said, loudly. "You have to leave now."

Finkel gasped. "Why did you just do that?" he snapped, furiously. "Why did you just say my name?"

"Don't raise your voice!" the young cop yelled.

But Finkel couldn't contain himself anymore. All the anger and frustration built up after years of feeling falsely persecuted exploded. "Look," he fumed, "I come here to make money. I'm not doing anything illegal. They've been taking money away from suckers all day. I put myself through school by using my brain! And I have to deal with these people threatening to assault me? Then I ask you not to say my name, and after I leave I'm sure you'll give everyone my information!"

The cops and the goon were silent. What was wrong with this kid? He was just some Jersey punk in foreign territory, a nobody, as far as they were concerned. They could snap his neck like a piece of okra and no one on the planet would know. "Your taxi's here," the older cop said. "Why don't you get in it and go?"

As Finkel headed off into the night, he had two words for Shreveport: good riddance. Finkel had had bad swings before, of course, it was part of any game. One week alone, the Lawyers dropped $300,000 in the casinos. Usually, Finkel could ride out the swings; it was one of his best traits. But there was only so much that even he could take.

During a trip to an Indian reservation in the Midwest, Finkel went to cash out his $23,000 winnings, only to be told that his chips could not be redeemed. "If you want to get them cashed," the clerk said, "you have to go to the Tribal Gaming Commission and lodge a complaint." Finkel stormed across the street to the Tribal Gaming Commission's office. It was in the same building as the police department, not a good sign.

"We've got a complaint against you guys," the chief of police told Finkel. "Put your hands against the wall." Finkel protested as they patted him down and led him into a back room. "We've been told you're perpetrating a fraud," the cop said.

"How have we been doing that?" Finkel gasped.

"That's still being investigated. We need to confiscate those chips while the investigation is going on."

"Can't we just leave now?"

"No, we'll have to arrest you."

"For what?"

"For resisting arrest. You have two options. You either give us your chips or we'll confiscate your rental car with all your possessions and you can sit in the cell while you think about it."

"What the fuck?" Finkel cried. "You're police officers! You're supposed to be impartial! And we haven't committed a crime here!"

"It's tribal land," the chief said. "The law is what we say it is."

Finkel slumped his shoulders. It was like an absurd scene out of a Kafka novel. Here he was, once again, being beaten down by the system simply for being too smart. If you're smart in America, it seemed, you had to play by certain rules. As a kid, you had to be quiet, not show up the others, stay in the woodwork. As an adult, you had to fall in line, get a job on Wall Street, in academics, or any other "legit" institution. But whose rules were these? Who decided how he had to play? Athletes could play pro ball and no one would bat an eye. Finkel and his friends were simply ahead of the curve, cutting the mold for a new kind of professional athlete. Why was being a cardplayer somehow bogus?

Fuck it! he thought. He wasn't going to take this like a rock. He was going on tilt, big-time. If these cops wanted to take his hard and honestly earned money, then they could keep the chips and shove them up their asses. He'd get a lawyer and force them to cough it up, which is precisely what he did after three long months of legal wrangling.

Finkel got his money back, after all. But the verdict was in: his days as a card counter were over. It was time to take down another game.

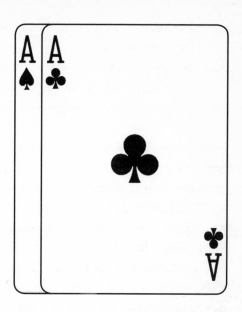

10. ALL-IN

At first glance, the World Poker Tour's Bellagio Five Diamond World Poker Classic in May 2002 seemed like any other big game.

All the most renowned poker stars were filing past the fountains into the Bellagio Casino in Las Vegas. The legendary Doyle Brunson, the two-time World Series of Poker cowboy from the 1970s, traded jibes with Chris Ferguson, the Ph.D. computer scientist whose long hair and beard earned him the nickname Jesus. "Action" Dan Harrington, the gray-haired 1995 World Series Champ, brushed elbows with the cocky sunglasses-wearing star Phil Helmuth.

In total, 145 players coughed up $10,000 for five days of No Limit Hold 'Em to compete for their share of the $1,416,200 prize pool. As the remaining six players gathered at the final table, they barely noticed the lipstick cameras staring up at their facedown cards. But those cameras were about to change the game in ways they could never imagine.

Hoping to cash in on the craze for reality television, the Travel Channel struck a deal with the World Poker Tour to attempt the seemingly impossible: make poker a spectator sport. But the problem was obvious. What fun is it to watch a game without seeing the players' cards? Without that vantage point, it's as dull as watching a group of guys staring into space.

With the lipstick cameras focused on each hidden hand, however, the audience could be in on all the drama: the bluffs, the tells, the check-raises, the folds. As billionaire Steve Lipscomb, founder of the World Poker Tour, trumpeted in a press release, "Poker is a stylish mix of strategy, psychology and showmanship. When you add sixteen cameras, a '[Who Wants to Be a] Millionaire'—style set, a live audience, and play-by-play analysis, it becomes as exciting to television viewers as it is to the players."

He was right. First airing in March 2003, the thirteen-week World Poker Tour series, which chronicled the tour from Costa Rica to Los Angeles, quickly became the highest-rated show on the channel. With a neon blue and red set, swaggering competitors, and, whenever possible, a sexy blonde hostess in a sarong, the WPT productions became a gambler's version of the World Wrestling Federation. Most remarkably, the show had legs. The more the Travel Channel repeated the episodes, the more viewers tuned in. What other sporting event gained viewers in *reruns*?

Lipscomb understood why viewers would watch poker tournaments over and over again, even when they knew the outcome. In the NFL or NBA, couch potatoes watch games as pure spectators. But poker, by nature, is an accessible game. Viewers aren't shut out of the action. For $10,000 they, too, could be sitting at the table at the Bellagio, playing against the legends of the game. With millions of people playing in weekly poker nights in homes around the country, every poker show on TV was a portal into a fantasy world that was waiting just for them.

While poker had been an American pastime forever, now the

media was catching up—and cashing in. In May 2003, after the main event of the World Series of Poker, it exploded. That's when a chubby twenty-seven-year-old restaurant accountant from Nashville, Tennessee, came out of seemingly nowhere to walk away with the top prize of $2.5 million. Everything about him—from his serendipitous name, Chris Moneymaker, to his back story—made him poker's own Cinderfella.

Though Moneymaker was among the legions of guys tuning in every week for the World Poker Tour broadcasts, he had little in the way of poker chops. A hard-partying amateur sports bettor while at the University of Tennessee, he didn't pick up the game until after he graduated. By then, he was married, over $50,000 in debt (largely from bad bets), and barely able to afford to play in the twenty-five-cent poker tables online. When he scrounged together $40 to enter an online tournament at Pokerstars.com, he didn't even want to win the top prize—a free $10,000 seat at the World Series of Poker; he would have preferred snagging the $8,000 fourth-place prize to help pay off his credit card bills.

Like it or not, Moneymaker indeed won the free Series spot, and soon found himself on the other side of the cameras at Binion's main event in Vegas. It was his first ever live tournament. With his baseball cap pulled down low and his shades hiding his nervous eyes, Moneymaker tried to keep his poker face while playing against Johnny Chan, Phil Ivey, Howard "The Professor" Lederer, and other legends he recognized from TV. It wasn't easy. At one point, he got so worked up in trying to stare down the Professor and Chan that he forgot his turn to bet. "You know it's up to you, right?" said Chan. Moneymaker, with all the ESPN viewers watching, turned bright red and mucked his cards.

But no sooner did he get branded the archetypal Internet fish than he started finding his groove. First he knocked out Chan; then he busted Ivey. And, in the end, he got the cards—and necessary moments of courage—to outlast them all. The ultimate regular Joe prevailed to take the $2.5 million prize and championship bracelet. If the poker world was shocked, Moneymaker could barely believe it himself. It was, he would later write, "more money than I had a right to even dream about. And much, much more than enough to justify the rip-roarin', stupid, shit-faced, I-should-be-ashamed-of-myself-but-for-the-fact-that-it-was-a-kick-ass-good-time drunk that came next. Abso-friggin'-lutely!"

By the time his buddies peeled him off the airport carpet and loaded him into the plane, the word was out. Poker really was the people's game. Moneymaker's underdog victory, broadcast repeatedly on ESPN, sent a clear message to the amateurs around the planet: if this nobody from Nashville could parlay his online game into a World Series bracelet, then anyone could win.

Legions of wannabe Moneymakers took to the online poker sites to live their wildest dreams. When they arrived, Jonny Magic and the card shark kids were waiting to crush them.

The sun was coming up over the inflatable pink flamingoes outside the basement window, and Jordan Berkowitz was still wide awake. It was a Wednesday morning in Media, Pennsylvania, a woodsy burg of McMansions outside Philly. Jordan hadn't slept in two days. He was pacing his wood-paneled room. Mentholated nicotine raced through his veins. Newport ashes freckled his gray Tommy Hilfiger socks. And his ordinarily spiky gelled coif was matted from futile time on the pillow.

After just winning $72,000 playing poker online, it's hard to crash. Jordan was an Internet card shark. He spent his long days—and nights—milking hundreds of thousands of dollars from the chumps online. "They suck so bad," he scoffed, "it's like playing with babies." Jordan was only seventeen.

Technically, he wasn't supposed to be gambling at all. On Poker-stars.com, one of the sites where he plied his trade, players must be eighteen years of age or older to ante up. But since dropping out of high school to gamble full-time, Jordan had help getting around the restriction. It came from his mom, who let him gamble under her name and the joint bank account they shared. "I'd rather he get an education," said Pagona Berkowitz, a single mother and painting contractor, "but I'm not stopping him. He's my son. I can't let him fall on his face."

Under the mother-son arrangement, Jordan was permitted to gamble online however much—whenever, wherever—he wanted as long as he helped pay the bills. His winnings—$300,000 and climbing—went into the joint account, from which he drew his allowance.

"I buy more shit than you can possibly imagine," said Jordan, who sported diamond earrings and a wardrobe piled with Sean John tracksuits. His ride was a $35,000 jet black Infiniti G35 with a $10,000 stereo, neon green tube lighting, and a revolving supply of $2,000, twenty-inch spinners. "I've had like three of these fuckers stolen, but I just keep buying them," he said.

Jordan wasn't the only kid cashing in. He was part of an emerging generation of cardplayers who were making a killing in online gambling. They didn't come from nowhere. They came from Magic. Jordan had been traveling the Magic Pro Tour since he was fourteen, and had used his $40,000 in winnings to bankroll his new poker career. But of all the Magic players storming the Internet, none had accumulated a $1 million bankroll like the hero Jordan had grown up admiring, Jonny Magic.

Finkel began venturing online more frequently around the time he decided to leave the card-counting team. Frustrated with life on the road and the hassles of casino personnel, he turned to the Internet, where he could apply his skills to crushing the competition—and never even have to leave his house.

For Finkel and his Magic crew, unlike most of the population, online gambling was nothing new. They had begun venturing into Internet poker rooms shortly after their collective *Rounders* epiphany in 1998. The online poker environment felt strikingly familiar for a kid reared on video games and Magic cards. The sites dressed up their action with video game superfluities: sound effects of rattling chips, goofily animated characters seated at a card table, and a disembodied voice that announces "good job!!" when a player wins a hand.

With the strategic minds of card veterans and the hand-eye reflexes of expert video gamers, the Magic crew locked on target. To maximize their winnings, they played four tables online at a time, clicking back and forth between games: raising bets, folding bad cards, and raking in chips. With the unlimited access, 24/7, the Internet became an assembly line of poker fish. Tired of sluggish offline games, players could undertake as many as 500 hands an hour.

At a real table in the real world players can pick up on an opponent's tells, physical signs that give away a bluff, or, even worse, a great hand. Without these cues online, the Magic players focused on betting patterns—noting, for example, how often someone limped in and made a huge reraise, even though they didn't have Aces. For those who couldn't keep patterns in their noggins, programs were made up to automatically log hand histories.

Just as they were getting their game on, as fate would have it, the Moneymaker dam broke, unleashing rivers of fish into their pool. Since U.S. laws against Internet casinos have no impact on the offshore operations that run the sites, the numbers skyrocketed from 1,500 to 15,000 players per hour. An estimated 15 million players were betting $3.2 million every day online for a total of $1.2 billion per year. So much for working at Domino's; for the card shark kids there was a very good living to be made.

Droves of Magic players made the migration: the guys from the Clowns—Dave Price, Ben, Eric—as well as some of Finkel's old Magic cohorts—David Williams, Thomas Keller, and even Finkel's old nemesis, David Bachmann of the Jersey Kids. But while Finkel watched his friends cash in, he quickly grew bored with the online game. The hours were long. The work, compared to Magic, blackjack, and even live poker games, was monotonous. Most of the time, he'd just be sitting there folding hands. But, as he soon discovered, there was another way, more lucrative and more interesting, to cash in with his computer. He didn't have to bet just poker. He could also bet sports.

Finkel got recruited to bet sports by Alex, who had become his closest mentor and friend. Alex, unlike Finkel, had barely any interest in sports as a fan, but saw sports betting as reminiscent of his options trading days. Together with another guy from the Lawyers, he developed a system that, when applied to the available lines, could give them roughly a 1 to 2.5 percent edge on all their bets. Finkel, the lifelong sports fan, wanted in.

The opponents in this game were the bookmakers, the people making the lines for everything from professional football to golf. Before a given game, Alex explained, you might have a choice between betting an underdog getting 7 points or an underdog getting 6.5 points; the price is the same. If you get 7 points, that means you have to bet $110 to win $100, whereas if you take 6.5 points you have to bet $100 to win $100. The question is: which is the better bet? If you knew how often a team in such a line wins by exactly seven, you can figure out which is better.

The answer, Alex said, could be found through two of Finkel's favorite subjects: math and history. Alex built a database that showed how teams performed against a variety of lines over dozens of years. "It turns out laying 11 to 10 and taking 7 points is slightly better than taking 6.5 points," Alex said. "The fraction of time they actually lose by specifically 7 is roughly 5 percent, so if you do the math, you do slightly better on the long run if you take 7 points. You can figure out historically how often certain events happen and use that as a prediction for the future."

Finkel was hooked, and the two formed a partnership. Alex would run the database, churning out the historical data, and Finkel would analyze that data to make bets. They rarely bet on full games. Instead, they wagered on halves or on propositions—such as how many sacks might be in a game or who was going to make the first touchdown or field goal. On a given game, they might have as many as five to ten bets. Betting on every game in a given day could mean more than a hundred bets a day. The analysis was key, since there were dozens of lines available, and the bookmakers varied in quality. Finkel had to make the call, often on the fly, about how to bet based on the incomplete information. It was just like old times.

By 2004, Finkel and Alex had doubled their income to a couple hundred grand each. Sports betting was challenging, lucrative, and, for Finkel, fun. While his friends cashed in on poker, he stuck with his game.

Then one day, for the hell of it, he joined them in trying to win a seat to the 2004 World Series of Poker in Las Vegas. This was expected to be the biggest year ever, with more than three times the number of competitors as the year before, and a total purse of over $20 million. Finkel entered an online tournament and, sure enough, won himself a free $10,000 seat.

As talk of the Series spread among the Magic players online, it turned out that the event was going to be something like a class reunion for the Magic kids—dozens of whom were now making a living playing poker. Between the Internet and Moneymaker and the World Poker Tour on TV, the old game was changing. Maybe now it was time for a new guard of players to take up the reins.

heroes' Reunion

Instant

Target player gains 7 life.

"You helped save my people from a Phyrexian fate. Did you think I wouldn't return the favor?"
—Eladamri, to Gerrard

Illus. Terese Nielsen
©1993–2000 Wizards of the Coast, Inc. 250/350

11. THE FINAL TABLE

Vegas is a town built on propositions. And over the years, as even ESPN has reported, there have been plenty of legendarily crazy bets.

One poker pro offered a vegetarian $10,000 to eat a hamburger, and lost. Another bet a friend $10,000 that he couldn't float in the ocean for twenty-four hours, and won. One guy wagered $30,000 that his buddy couldn't last thirty days in Des Moines, Iowa; his friend survived just two weeks and settled for $5,000. One of the most famous bets came when a poker player bet a male friend $100,000 to get breast implants; he lost, and his friend, to everyone's surprise, decided to keep the boobs.

But maybe the toughest bet is surviving the World Series of Poker. The game was a ballbuster from the start. It began in 1949 when a fifty-seven-year-old high roller named Vinny "the Greek" Dandalos stormed into Vegas looking for what he called "the biggest game this world has to offer." Benny Binion, owner of the Horseshoe Casino downtown, answered the call, and set up a heads-up match between the Greek and Johnny Moss, a poker champ from Texas.

Binion positioned them at a table near the front of the casino, and, like true gamers, they played for five months straight—pausing to sleep only every four or five days. The crowds were almost as tough as the players, watching obsessively until Moss finally took home $2 million and the win. Twenty-one years later, Binion re-created the big game, which he dubbed the World Series of Poker. By the next year's event, in 1971, the rules were in place. For $10,000, anyone could buy a seat in the No Limit Hold 'Em main event. The game would go on until there was just one person remaining at the table with a skyscraping tower of chips.

In 1970, with only six players competing, the odds against winning weren't bad. Times changed. By 2003, the year the World Poker Tour hit TV, 839 players came to play. After Moneymaker's fairy-tale win, a record 2,576 players either bought or won a $10,000 seat for the main event in May 2004.

The World Series of Poker was about to dole out $5 million to its champion, more than the first-place purses of Wimbledon, the Masters, and the Kentucky Derby combined. The second-place winner would take home the tidy sum of $3.5 million. And with nearly $35 million more on the line in the five-week Series' other thirty-three events, the promise of Vegas was bigger and brighter than ever. "Anyone can win!" was Binion's slogan. In a pool of players this big, even the best players admitted they'd need some luck to make the trip to the final table—and they'd need guts to survive.

As Finkel rode down the neon strip of Vegas for the first time in a year and a half, he had several reasons to feel gutsy. At one time or another, after all, he'd taken down every single casino he passed: Treasure Island, the Luxor, MGM Grand, the Paris. And, unlike many of the players entering the World Series of Poker, he had literally grown up at card tournaments. He'd been sitting for hours under hot lights concentrating on his hands since his teens.

The World Series was as much a contest of stamina as anything else. Some days, the contestants would be competing for as long as twelve hours at a time, subsisting on little more than cigarettes and Coke. There's only so long that someone can sit in one place and concentrate without going batty and losing feeling in his limbs. But for a generation of gamers who'd grown up on Magic and Nintendo, numbness was second nature. Plus, Finkel's lifetime of cards had imbued him with an unwavering sense of discipline. While it was important to have the smarts and strategic skills to play poker correctly, he had to have the wherewithal to make the right moves—without giving in to temptation or, worse, going on tilt.

But there was one major challenge for Finkel: he had to do all of this without the benefit of the Finkel Fear Factor. In Vegas, as far as Doyle Brunson and the other poker veterans were concerned, Finkel was prey—and so were the kid's friends.

In the past few years, Finkel was hardly the only Magic player who'd developed an interest in poker. Many of the top players on the Pro Tour scene were now, unbeknownst to many, making six figures a year playing poker, mainly online. Tournaments, however, were relatively new territory for the group. Just one Magic player had staked a flag here before. In 2002, Chris Pikula, a former teammate of Finkel's on the Dead Guys who now worked on Wall Street, made the final table of a $1,500 Limit Hold 'Em Shootout at the World Series of Poker. Though Pikula won only $3,700, his tenth-place showing caused a stir among the veteran poker scribes.

"If it's true, this is a great story," gushed one poker writer. "Chris Pikula claims that this is his first poker tournament ever. Imagine making a WSOP Final Table in your first tournament?" A Magic player online retorted: "Pikula probably forgot to mention that he has had success in other tournaments, where he pretends to be a powerful spellcaster who travels dominia challenging other mages to wonderous duels."

As Finkel's cab pulled up to a mansion in the suburbs of town, he was eager to reconvene with the old spellcasters once again. Several Magic guys had flown into town to stay at a sprawling estate owned by the parents of player Bob Maher. Each would have his own apartment and free use of the two pools, tennis court, and palatial grounds. Late into the night, he hung around the mansion with his buddies, smoking cigarettes and catching up. It was clear that the wizards were storming the series this year by force.

One of the early favorites to succeed was Thomas "Thunder" Keller. A hulking twenty-three-year-old with bleach-blond curls and a fiery tangle of hair on his chubby chin, Keller and his identical twin brother, Shawn, came of age on the Magic Pro Tour circuit. At seventeen, after scoring a 1580 on his SATs, Thomas, a classically trained pianist, left high school early after receiving a presidential scholarship to Stanford. While studying economics, however, he joked that his real major was poker.

Keller parlayed his strategic cardplaying skills by crushing the local card rooms. By the time he graduated from Stanford, he told his parents, a professor and a publishing executive, that he was going to be a professional player. Though disappointed, they couldn't argue with his winnings; Keller made as much in a day as some of his friends made in a year. Plus, he was happy. A few weeks before the World Series, Finkel and several other Magic guys attended Keller's wedding. With his new wife's blessing, Keller cut his honeymoon in Maui short to make sure he'd be in Vegas in time for the Series to begin.

Another Magic player had just driven in from a Magic tournament in San Diego to be in Vegas for the main event: Finkel's old friend David Williams. Like Finkel, Williams had filled out into an attractive young man. He had a neatly trimmed beard, a confident swagger, and a knockout girlfriend. Though Williams had once looked up to Finkel as the older, more experienced pro, he had long since come into his own. Known for his competitiveness and thoughtful play, he worked the underground clubs around Dallas. Drawing on his years of experience playing cards, his mathematical precision, and his years of tournament play, Williams cleaned up. Soon he was one of the many guys making six figures a year at poker. When he went to the mall and treated himself to a $400 pair of Prada sunglasses, he joked to a friend: "These are my poker glasses, I'm going to wear them at the World Series one day."

Now, after winning a $10,000 seat at the Series in an online tournament, Williams was heading with Finkel, Keller, and the rest to Binion's. And he was taking his shades with him.

When Finkel stepped onto Fremont Street, Vegas Vic, the forty-foot neon cowboy above the Pioneer Club, winked at him like an old friend. The last time Finkel had been at the flashing intersection in front of Binion's Horseshoe Casino, he had been costumed like Vic's cheesy cousin, cloaked in a big black cowboy hat and shiny *Playboy* shirt. That was the night he squeezed the casino across the street, the Four Queens, for $90,000.

But this evening, as the crowd swarmed under the flashing blue neon lights of Binion's, he had no reason to hide. He wore his standard apparel: backward Phillies cap, two silver hoop earrings, and baggy jeans. His T-shirt showed a picture of George H. W. Bush and George W. Bush, with the words "Dumb and Dumber" underneath. On top he wore his favorite hooded sweatshirt, a black zip-up with the words "Battle School," an homage to his favorite sci-fi novel, *Ender's Game,* stitched across the front. He had never been here looking more like himself. And as the throngs of people swarmed into Binion's, he had never been more ready to play.

Compared to the palatial and glitzy casinos on the strip, Binion's, like most of the casinos downtown, retained the Old Vegas spirit. It felt like he was walking into an old cigar. Brown ceiling fans slowly stirred the stale air. Red velvety wallpaper clung precariously to the walls. Broken slot machines rotted darkly along the walls. Brittle doughnuts and slimy bowls of fruit salad lined the display case of the Snack Bar.

The real action was happening in the back, where poker was under way. The closer Finkel got to the room, the louder the old familiar rattle of chips became, like plastic rain falling on a bamboo roof. The players sat at their posts. In the corner, an old brown cart with the word "Horseshoe" on the side bore big glass jugs of Tangerine Sours, Good and Plentys, and Super Chickles, available for a quarter. Asian women kneaded weary gamblers in their $1-per-minute massage chairs. Red electronic letters streamed along a digital strip with the phrase "Millions are played. Legends are made."

Along one section of wall hung the Gallery of Champions, a display of framed photos of the previous World Series champions. Finkel ran his eyes over the familiar faces of the winners—Johnny Moss, Doyle Brunson, Johnny Chan, Dan Harrington, Chris Moneymaker—many of whom were there in the flesh around the tables today. Finally his eyes came to the one spot in the lower right-hand corner that was empty, waiting for the new champ who would be crowned at the end of the Series.

Not surprisingly, the Vegas odds makers were putting the money on veterans like Brunson and Harrington to take the prize. "Ten years ago there was a hundred people in the tournament; they were all top-quality players," Brunson sniffed during an ESPN interview, "whereas seventy-five percent of players here are relatively weak."

Finkel sat down at his assigned seat alongside guys twice his age. Though he hadn't had to put up any of his own money to compete in the World Series, he was as vested as anyone. As the cards fell, he reached for his chips. At the poker table, players expressed themselves, in part, by how they handled their chips. Some rolled their chips, somersaulted them through their fingers, or stacked them high to impress others. Others counted them at every opportunity, a sign of weakness, maybe, or strength.

Many players, particularly at such a big event, brought good-luck charms to accessorize their stacks. Grown men clutched stuffed animals; others propped up pictures of their kids. Johnny Chan, the World Series champ, was renowned for palming a good-luck orange. One new player, Greg Raymer, toted around lucky fossils and wore a pair of holographic glasses he bought at the Tower of Terror ride at Disney. The glasses gave him a permanent stare that, he hoped, would bring him some added magic.

Finkel didn't believe in such charms. Instead, he just riffled his chips, splitting them into two stacks and expertly shuffling them together with his fingertips. It was a move perfected after hundreds of hours at the blackjack tables, and it had a suitably intimidating effect, particularly compared to Internet players, many of whom never fingered a real chip in their lives.

As the play proceeded, Finkel followed the protocol he'd developed since his days back at the Diamond Club in New York. Though he didn't play nearly as much poker as he used to, his mind and fingers reflexively fell back into the groove. Raise. Check-raise. Fold. The chips came and went. Around him, players would bust out around the tournament, dying with a groan or yelp as if they'd stepped on land mines. But Finkel was all alone, in the zone, plowing through the jungle and watching where he stepped.

If the other players weren't busting out, they were going on tilt. The pressure just to play in the World Series was enormous, particularly for guys who considered poker their living. "You're talking fear, greed, anger, elation," as Harrington put it to ESPN, "and if you don't control it, you're going to be a loser." One player, Mike "the Mouth" Matasow, lost his cool so many times that the "Mike Matasow Blow Up" was named for him. At one point, he craned over Greg "Fossilman" Raymer, spitting the words "Don't mess with me, buddy. I'll bust you! I have big cojones! You have small cojones!" But his cojones couldn't keep him from busting out.

While others dropped around him, Finkel remained cool. Before he knew it, four hours had passed and he was still alive. But the blows came. After flopping the top two pair, he bet three-quarters of the pot, only to be taken down on the river by a guy with a flush. Finkel shook his head and moved to his next hand, with only $3,000 in chips remaining.

Sitting in the last position, he found himself holding pocket Queens—a good hand by any stretch. There was $2,000 in the pot. He risked $1,000, and found himself heads up with a heavyset amateur who had been bluffing his way through ridiculous hands so far. But, this being poker, Finkel didn't celebrate yet. The flop came: King, 7, 5. The big man checked, Finkel checked. The turn card was a 2. No help. The big man checked, Finkel checked. The river was another blank, a card that didn't help Finkel. The big man took a long look across the table, as Finkel riffled his chips. Then he bet $3,000. If Finkel was going to play, he'd have to risk everything and go all-in.

There are crossroads in every person's life, Finkel knew, billions of tiny decisions that can alter history. Cross the street and get hit by a bus. Introduce yourself to the person you'll marry. Poker, or just about any card game for that matter, is an elegant distillation of this experience. When Finkel first started playing cards, he made the decisions like a boy—tentative, thoughtless, weak. As he grew up, the games made his decisions sharper, more confident. Before long, it was this ability to make quick decisions based on incomplete information that defined him as a champion. And it was the maturity to accept his decisions, and the cards he was dealt, that transformed him.

Finkel reached for his chips, and pushed them into the center of the table. The big man turned over his cards to reveal a King, giving him the top pair. Finkel was done.

But, as he rose from the table, he didn't sulk. He had spent the past decade proving to himself and his peers that even the unlikeliest underdog can find the courage, in life and in play, to go all-in. As his sister, Jenny, wryly put it, "You're the poster boy for a generation of losers; you're showing that they can be successful, too."

And, with their hero watching, the kids were about to prove it.

Hollywood Mike May, Finkel's poker mentor from the Diamond Club, was leaving Binion's after a long day of playing when he got stopped by David Williams. Mike, who knew Williams through Finkel, could see the eagerness in the young player's eyes—and in the way he stood there in the shadow of Binion's with his proud mom, Shirley.

Though Williams had played cash games in the past, this was his first big tournament. "Hey, Mike," he said, "you have any advice?" Mike was tired, ready to save up his energy for the remaining days, but managed to offer one nugget he'd been told long ago. "It's such a long tournament," he said, "people are under such stress. You'll run into people who want to get out of their chair. They panic from stress and want to get knocked out and go home. They're like a drowning person. Don't let them pull you under."

Williams had reason to feel the pressure. A new cavalry was stampeding inside Binion's storied poker room. The first shots sounded when a twenty-three-year-old poker dealer named Scott Fischman became the youngest player ever to win two events. He outlasted Brunson and the other vets to win $300,000 in the $1,500 buy-in No Limit Hold 'Em event; three days later, he took $100,200 in a $2,000 buy-in.

Twenty-four hours later, another young cowboy made his play, this time in the $5,000 buy-in No Limit Texas Hold 'Em event. With a prize of $382,020 on the line, this was already one of the most competitive lineups yet; 253 players, including celebrities like Harrington, Moneymaker, and even Spider-Man himself, twenty-eight-year-old actor Tobey Maguire, sat down to play. The ESPN cameramen were blindsided when a pudgy, boy-faced twenty-three-year-old with a fiery chin-beard outlasted them all to make it to the final table. His name was Thunder Keller, Finkel's old Magic buddy. And he played like a wizard.

With the cameras rolling, Keller made it to the final two, going heads-up against a professional player from Stockholm named Martin "the Knife" de Knijff. The dealer dealt him pocket tens. Keller gulped, and made his usual raise—three times the big blind, or, in this case, $24,000. The Knife called, and the flop came: 9-4-2 with two clubs. Keller gulped again, as his heart pounded in his ribs. Feeling confident with his overpair, two cards higher than anything on the table, he made a big bet, almost the size of the pot. The Knife sharpened, pushing his chips all-in. Keller called.

After years on the Magic circuit, Keller had developed a sixth sense for reading players. He figured that unless the Knife had a set, three of a kind, he'd be the winner. But when the Knife turned his cards, revealing a King and 2 of clubs, Keller thought his powers might have failed him. If the turn and river cards came up a club, deuce, or King, he was toast. The dealer discarded or burned the next card, and showed the turn: a 9. Keller had two pair. And the river came up another 9, giving him a full house, and the title. Keller leapt in the air, pumping his ham-sized fists for the ceiling.

The reporters swarmed the doughy kid, who amazed them by revealing that this was his first trip to the Series. "The Internet is a great teaching tool," Thunder said, giving props to his Magic buddies online. "The players there don't get enough respect."

But they would soon enough. All across the poker room, Finkel's Magic cowboys kept firing. In the $1,500 Limit Hold 'Em Shoot Out, twenty-two-year-old Magic player Brock Parker made the final table, finishing third. Before long, seven of the twenty-five gold bracelet winners were in their twenties, five of whom were under twenty-five. It was the highest number of young champs in the history of the Series. Though there had certainly been individual young stars in the past—such as Stu Ungar and Phil Ivey—there had never been such a mass infiltration. "This has become the 'Year of the Young Guns,'" a reporter declared. "Has poker now passed the proverbial torch from one generation to the next?"

The answer could only come from one place: the final table of the main event. And, after battling his way to the top, David Williams was heading there. He wasn't the only Magic player in the mix. Williams was joined by Mattias Andersson, a gawky twenty-four-year-old who had won the 2001 Magic National championship in his home country of Sweden. At the World Series, he got dubbed the "screaming Swede" for the way he leapt from the table and yelled "daaaaaaahhhhhh!" with every win.

As word of Andersson's and Williams's ascension to the final table spread in Magic chat rooms online, the community around the world tuned in. Richard Garfield was padding across his sprawling home office in mismatched socks when he got the news. From his sprawling mansion on the shores of Lake Washington in Seattle, Garfield, like millions of card buffs around the world, had been following the Series on the Web. The guys at Wizards crowded around their PCs. Magic players swarmed their computers. A couple even flew to Vegas to watch the action begin.

The fact that two of the final nine players were from Magic was no small feat. One by one, the suckers, legends, and celebs had dropped. Hollywood's poker star Ben Affleck bit the dust. Even Brunson was sent hobbling out on his crutch as the room burst into respectful applause. Yet of the less than ten Magic players who entered the tournament, two had outlasted 2,574 others to make it all the way to the end. It didn't take long for the poker players to start sniffing out more about this weird game called Magic.

"Is there something that we nongathering poker players are missing?" one poker player posted online.

"My son plays MTG [Magic: The Gathering], and most of the best players tend to be game geeks," replied another.

"I guess if you want your son/daughter to be good at poker," mused someone else, "start them playing Magic at like 8."

"A lot of the new faces in high level internet poker seem to have some kind of Magic . . . experience," responded another. "I have no idea what these games are like or even how they are played, but I am assuming these games involve some kind of analytical gameplay that prepares the player to adapt to poker very well. It will be interesting to see if this trend continues and the traditional dungeons and dragons type stereotypical 'geeks' (not trying to be offensive) are going to start a new wave in poker."

Joining Andersson and Williams at the final table were two other young guns in their twenties, and one certifiable legend, Action Dan Harrington, the fifty-seven-year-old champion who had won the 1995 World Series. This was the second year in a row that Action Dan had made the final table, an unprecedented feat that the poker pundits described as the greatest accomplishment ever in the game. The chip leader, however, was Greg "Fossilman" Raymer, who, like Williams, had won a seat online.

Compared to Raymer, a portly, balding thirty-nine-year-old wearing a string of lucky shark teeth and goofy holographic eyeball glasses, Williams, dressed in a black button-up shirt and stealth wraparound shades, already looked like a star. And he had the fans to prove it. Finkel stood by the rail with a crowd of other Magic players, including Mark Justice, the "stormin' Mormon" who dominated the Pro Tour back when Finkel got his start. They all wanted to see one of their own make good, and prove to the world, and the poker elite, that their time had finally come. "This one," Williams thought, "is for the gamers."

After every big hand, Williams would give his mother a big hug as she clutched her lucky stuffed animal. "When you travel with your mother," the ESPN reporter quipped, "it sure doesn't intimidate the other players." But as the reporter watched, other players, including Andersson, fell to the wayside. Williams managed to hang on to become one of the final four. To pump up the drama, a procession of casino employees came out with cardboard boxes full of the main prize: $5 million in cash. As they stacked the bricks up on the table, Williams asked Harrington, "When you won, did you just bring it out in a big bag or what happened?"

Action Dan gave him a grandfatherly smile and replied, "I just had them reduce it to a check." But inside he was getting ready to pounce. As he told an ESPN reporter earlier, "I don't care how nonchalant they act, they're intimidated by me being at the table. It gives me a huge edge."

Before long, the blade pointed Williams's way. Harrington put Williams all-in on the following hand. But when Williams caught a full house on the river card, the crowd erupted. Harrington, who had been bluffing, was gone. Williams had just put the last legend of the tournament to pasture. "It's an honor to play with you," Williams whispered to a shaken Action Dan, as Finkel and the other guys burst into cheers. "This is No Limit Texas Hold 'Em," the ESPN announcer said, "but no Texan since Doyle Brunson has won. Dave could be the next Texan to win."

Then came his chance. Williams was sitting across the felt from just one other player: the big man with holographic eyes, Greg "Fossilman" Raymer. "We're down to two," the ESPN reporter announced to the viewers, "David, and the Goliath of this table." Off camera, it was clear who many people wanted to win. A quiet voice of another staffer whispered in Williams's ear before the final match. "Please beat this fat motherfucker," he said.

Finkel and the Magic guys rushed to the rail. Garfield and the others around the Net hovered over their PCs. Williams's mom clutched her lucky doll. At the very least, Williams was going to walk away with $3.5 million, but at this point, it was all about the win. Six hands passed without event, until Williams found himself sitting with an Ace 4, unsuited. He opened with a bet of $300,000. Raymer called. The flop came up with a 5, 4, and 2. Raymer checked, and Williams bet another $500,000. Raymer responded by raising $1.1 million more. Williams called.

As another 2 came up on the turn, Raymer grabbed a fat stack of chips and pushed in $2.5 million. Williams called again. He wasn't backing down. When the river came up another 2, Williams had a full house. When Raymer went all-in, he didn't flinch. "Call," he said, throwing down his cards. But Raymer had pocket 8s, getting the higher full house.

"Yeah!" Fossilman yelped, as the room burst into cheers.

Williams stood there, stunned. The Holy Grail was right there in his grasp, he thought, and then it dropped away. All those old feelings of loss and disappointment crashed down again, sweeping him under. He didn't think about how he'd spend his millions or talk with the reporters or hug his girlfriend or mom. He just thought about how he failed.

Then, out of the crowd, came a hand. It was Finkel, there to re-assure his friend as always. David might have lost to Goliath this time, but, for everyone on the rails, it was a win.

12. THE ONLY GAME IN TOWN

"Argentina! Australia! Austria! Belgium!" The announcer's voice boomed over a techno backbeat as the opening ceremony began. One by one, the 301 competitors marched through a crowd of cheering fans, hoisting the flags of the fifty-six countries they represented. "Switzerland! Ukraine! Uruguay! United States!"

But these were no ordinary athletes. The champ from Brazil was an overstuffed guy with glasses in a Superman T-shirt. The Irishman resembled an Amish Burl Ives. And the guy from the Netherlands appeared to be schlepping his laptop. As Kyle Murray, brand manager of Magic at Wizards of the Coast, joked, "It's an Olympics of the mind."

The players had road-tripped here to San Francisco on Labor Day weekend 2004 to compete for their share of $1 million in prizes at the Magic World Championships. In one corner of the auditorium, a woman sculpted a life-size dragon from aluminum foil. Over a mound of fries, two skinny kids debated the virtues of the Black Lotus card. Richard Garfield took the stage in mismatched socks, clasped his hands behind his back, and leaned tentatively into the microphone to give his opening remarks.

"If I were a composer, this would be like the world's best musicians coming together to play my music," he said. "But I'm not a composer, I'm a game designer. And I'm proud to be a game designer. Games are amazing things. They are training for your mind in the same way that sports are training for your body. It's that belief which has led me to convert my home into a mental gymnasium. My family is in constant training. You've heard of the Suzuki method for training children to play violin? Well, I'm using it to train gaming virtuosos, I hope. When I've taught them all I can, I'm going to send them off to train under Kai and under Finkel, then they'll be able to come here and see firsthand what makes this event so special as they compete against people from all over the world for days on end. Good luck. Play fair. And have fun."

As the players broke for their positions, a diminutive kid in a Korn T-shirt approached an older player in a Sean John tracksuit. "Hey, Dave," chirped the kid, "Dave Williams. You got the time?"

Williams flicked his wrist out from under his immaculate sleeve, revealing a glittering new Rolex. "It's about ten-thirty," he said, smoothly.

"There it is!" the kid cheered, pointing at Williams's wrist. "Nice watch, dude!"

"Thanks," Williams said, heading on his way. A few seconds later, another grinning kid asked him the time. Williams shook his head. "It's weird that everyone's shaking my hand," he commented to a friend. "I'm still the same person." But the watch told the gamers a different story. As the players knew from the gossip online, Williams bought the $20,000 Rolex the day after his World Series of Poker score.

In the few months that had passed since the main event, the members of the Magic community—like cardplayers around the world—were still reeling from the infiltration of young guns. With ESPN broadcasting the World Series around the clock, and garnering huge ratings, the mythological meeting of David and Goliath had firmly branded itself into the zeitgeist. This triggered a wave of hand-wringing in the press about the apparent rise of kid gamblers.

USA Today ran reports on the craze of teen poker nights, with players as young as ten who were "chilling and bluffing their way into the new year as a host of market indicators—and a good measure of mounting concern—speak to a stunning passion among young people for a game traditionally associated with gruff men and stinky cigars." The *New York Times* ran a page-one story with the headline "Poker Faces, and They Haven't Started Shaving." "Do you know where your high school kids are at night?" the story read. "If the answer is yes, chances are it's because they're poring over poker hands, practicing their dead man's stares, and aping the big-timers on ESPN sitting there with dark glasses and million-dollar piles of chips at the World Series of Poker in Las Vegas."

An editorial in *Newsday* weighed in: "It's bad enough that the federal government is saddling this generation of kids with a multitrillion-dollar debt and diminishing prospects for Social Security. The last thing they need is a gambling problem."

As Williams quickly discovered, the media wasn't alone in this concern. Back in Binion's just after the final hand, Williams conscientiously phoned the people at Wizards to see how they wanted him to answer the inevitable question about his origins. "How do you want me to play this? Should I mention Magic?" he asked. "Is this good for you guys? Or is this bad?"

On the other end of the line at Wizards, the staff raced for an answer. Though they were happy for Williams's victory, they sweated the potential public relations fallout. They didn't want parents who were dropping their fourteen-year-olds off at Magic tournaments to think their kids were hanging out with gamblers. "We'd rather not have you bring up the connection," Williams was told.

In the heat of the moment, Williams agreed to the plan. If the press asked where he came from, he wouldn't say Magic. He'd say Texas.

When Garfield, a lifelong poker player, later heard the news of this cover-up, he hit the roof. "This is ridiculous," he said. "We should embrace poker! Poker is a well-established game. At this point, everyone recognizes the game. Everyone recognizes the skill in poker! And having Magic tied to poker just legitimizes gaming as a whole."

He wasn't the only one burning to let the geek flag fly. "Wizards can hurt themselves by not seizing the opportunity to reframe their game as the greatest learning device in the history of the world," fumed former Magic pro Mike Long. "It's something that can teach your child to do anything at any speed! Dave's win is a metaphor that you can take the skills you learn in Magic and do whatever you want in life."

But of all the players, maybe none took more umbrage at the reactionary stance against Williams's win than Magic's biggest hero, Jon Finkel. There was a flaw in the argument that Magic could lead kids to gambling, he thought. "Poker is a game of skill," he said. "You don't see Magic players playing slots, because it's stupid. I place bets on sports and that's how I make a living. Is it gambling?" And that was the thing, he thought; this wasn't gambling. Their skill was in finding the edge to these games—Magic, poker, blackjack. And when you find the edge, you eliminate the gamble.

As the weeks passed, the skeptics at Wizards eventually came around to accept this point of view. Many of them were poker players, after all, just like the 50 million other Americans playing the game. After their initial misgivings, they decided to openly embrace Wizards' burgeoning clan of poker stars.

"Everyone now agrees we should leverage opportunities like this," said Wizards' Randy Buehler, who now hoped poker players might make the reverse commute to Magic's game. "The next time something like this happens," he said, "we're not going to tell the guy to cover it up." And with legions of Magic players eyeing the future World Series of Poker events, they figured that time would come soon enough. "This was Normandy," Buehler said, "and we stormed the beach." The greatest testament to Magic's enduring appeal was that millionaires like Williams and Finkel came back.

After four nonstop days of gaming, the Magic World Championship was finally winding down. The players' eyes were fireballs. Silvery card wrappers littered the floor. Off in the corner, the giant dragon sculpture was complete, presiding over the hall.

Nearby, Garfield ambled through the crowd. He was glad that the relationship between Magic and poker had found its peace. Like a proud father, he was happy to see both his game and its players grow up. "Every time I come to one of these big tournaments," he said, "I see less people who don't know how to groom themselves. I see people who are in better shape, people who take showers, who are less overweight, who are not hopelessly niche." He paused for a small gulp of air. "You can tell Magic is mainstream," he said, "because the players don't look like gamers anymore."

On stage, a curly-haired fifteen-year-old from Amsterdam named Julien Nuijten hoisted an enormous cardboard check for $52,366—the prize for winning the championship match; it was the most money awarded for a single game since Finkel walked away with $45,000 after the 2000 World Championship in Brussels. But Jonny Magic was seasoned enough to take it in stride. With lifetime Magic winnings of nearly $300,000, he was still at the top of the game, second only to Kai Budde, who had close to $350,000. And his archest rivals figured the old champ could come back if and when he was ready.

"Finkel's the most talented player in the game, more than me by far," Budde said. "If he wanted to really play again, I'm sure he could surpass me."

With the sun going down over the bay, Finkel stepped outside for a smoke. If he had to bet, he figured this was probably the last time all the old Magic guys would be together at an event. Times were changing. People were getting jobs, having families, settling down. Though Finkel sometimes questioned how much or how little he was contributing to the world, he was, as he said, "saving up for future generations of Finkels." And after all these years of competing, he was finally starting to appreciate what he'd done.

"When you're a teenager, you feel things so strongly," he said. "I'll never have a crush on a girl like I had crushes on girls when I was a teenager. I will never read a book that will profoundly move me like books moved me when I was a teenager. If I win the World Series of Poker, it will be nice, people will see me on the streets, but it will annoy me after a while. I'm not good at those awkward social encounters, like 'Hi, how are you?' I'm not gregarious like that. But, like, my life is already fine, it's a success. The World Series will just mean I have a bunch more money, but it won't ever compare."

As Finkel took the final drag on his cigarette, a group of his old Magic buddies filed out the door. They were going to go blow some money at a strip club, and wanted to know if Finkel wanted to tag along.

"No thanks," he said, and they went on their way. There was a new trading card game by Marvel that all the kids were playing, and Finkel wanted to give it a try. He put out his smoke and headed back inside. It was time to take down another game, even if it took all night.

EPILOGUE

In the wake of the young guns' stampede at the 2004 World Series of Poker, it became clear that a new generation of cardplayers was here to stay.

In 2005, poker continued its run as America's fastest-growing sport. ESPN showed World Series of Poker reruns around the clock. When NBC wanted something to go up against the Super Bowl pregame show on Fox, they broadcast a champion event from the World Poker Tour. With other channels following suit, it was hard to flip the station without seeing some celebrity or twenty-something kid in a baseball cap staring down the flop.

As players watched the action, they wanted to get in on it more than ever, too. Casinos bumped up the number of poker tables, increasing the tournaments and offering lessons for newbies. More and more amateurs plied their skills online, spending an estimated $4 billion on their games. There were poker video games, poker books, poker magazines, and, for an Elk lodge in Andover, Massachusetts, a poker-themed fund-raiser in lieu of the annual ball. "Poker themes are great for couples because men feel included," the local newspaper reported, "especially the ones who don't dance."

But, online and off, it was clear who ruled the new game. As one Web site put it, "Poker was always an 'Old-Boys Network.' Until 2004, that is. Now there's a 'young-boys network.' " And the leaders of the boys club were Jonny Magic and the card shark kids.

Shortly after David Williams's second-place finish at the World Series of Poker, word spread among cardplayers that he, in actuality, had proven to be the event's top money winner. Greg "Fossilman" Raymer revealed on poker newsgroups that a little more than 40 percent of his $5 million winnings had gone to investors who backed his play throughout the year. Raymer was left with around $3 million, $500,000 less than his competitor. A twenty-three-year-old Magic player, in other words, had become the most profitable tournament champ in the history of the game.

Williams proved to be more than a lucky hand, coming in first and second in subsequent events and becoming one of the sport's most popular players. *Playboy* magazine called him "the future of poker." Thomas "Thunder" Keller, the second-biggest Magic winner at the World Series, also continued his run on the circuit, including his appearance at the World Poker Tour's inaugural "Young Guns" event.

Other Magic players—Brock Parker, Kenneth Rose, Mattias Andersson—continued to make their presence known. In June 2005, Eric "Efro" Froehlich, a mountainous twenty-one-year-old Magic veteran and Finkel friend, would become the youngest player ever to earn a World Series of Poker championship bracelet. With his Magic buddies cheering him on, he beat over one thousand players in the $1,500-buy-in Limit Hold 'Em tournament to take $361,910. In his postgame interview, he told ESPN, "This win basically justifies my whole life."

With the word out, more and more poker players loudly wondered about this mysterious game that was breeding all these new stars. "Seems to me there are several recently successful live and online players who have played this Magic game at high levels," posted one player online. "I don't know anything about the game other than I had a weird roommate in college who played it and he had some weird friends that played with him. I kind of assumed it was like one of those D&D type games or something."

While the poker players sniffed out the Magic players, the smart, weird boys continued to sharpen, and exploit, their games. Magic had its biggest year ever, capitalizing on the fantasy craze to earn more than $125 million. At the same time, trading card games for the preteen set—including Pokemon, Duel Masters, and Yu-Gi-Oh!—lured millions of new players into the sport of cards every year. A system and culture were in place. Pokemon players would grow into Magic, then Magic players would grow into poker. The kids who used to be sidelined now had a culture in which they could refine their skills. The game of cards, after all these years, had become not only a sport, but a home.

As a future generation of mental athletes found their groove, Finkel made his next move. With $1 million in the bank, the twenty-six-year-old didn't need to find a new game. After his brief run at the World Series of Poker in 2004, he focused his energies on the live poker tournament arena. "I've got the itch," he said. And, true to form, it didn't take long for him to scratch it.

In January 2005, Finkel drove down to Atlantic City for a World Series of Poker circuit event at Harrah's. He hoped to win some cash and, once and for all, get himself ranked as a player on the professional poker scene. As he hit the road, he had reason to be optimistic. The Philadelphia Eagles were in the playoffs. He had been dating a leggy Russian knockout. He had quit smoking. He had just found an apartment with a fun-loving group of friends in Manhattan's West Village. And, thanks to Alex, his business partner and friend, he was already having his most lucrative week ever.

Hours before Finkel left his apartment, Alex came in second at the PokerStars Caribbean Adventure No Limit Hold 'Em event in the Bahamas to win $484,000. Because Finkel and Alex split all their gambling winnings 50/50, Finkel himself walked away with $242,000. Coupled with a huge day of sports betting, netting the two of them

$40,000, Finkel was on a roll. Within a few months, he would be up $800,000—well on his way, even considering potential losses, to a $2 million to $3 million year.

When he showed up at Harrah's for the circuit event, Finkel wasn't alone. He'd come with Eric Kesselman and a couple of other friends from the card-counting team. Though Finkel had left the Lawyers years before, he still maintained a friendship with the crew. The Lawyers, though smaller in numbers, were still in business, and preparing for a run this weekend at the Borgata next door. But first, like Finkel, they wanted to take down this game at hand.

Finkel walked into the poker room wearing his ever-present backward Phillies baseball cap, baggy jeans, a T-shirt that read "Your Retarded," and his Battle School sweatshirt. His dad, Mark, had driven down from upstate to see his son compete in the event.

The room was crowded with ninety-nine other players, each hoping to become the next big champ. As the chips rattled, the cards fell, and one by one, the players sauntered away with lowered heads. Ten hours later, there were only three left. Finkel, leaning forward on a red satin pillow while getting a scalp massage from a young Asian woman, was one of them. "Oh, what a surprise," Eric said sarcastically, when he saw his friend among the sole survivors, "Finkel is at the final table."

It wouldn't be Finkel's last appearance. After finishing third that night to win $5,445, he impressed the crowd the following day by storming the final table of the next No Limit event. This time he came in second out of 125 players, and took $50,000. In total, he finished the week up more than $300,000. He was also now officially ranked on the race for cardplayer of the year. And with more poker tournaments on the horizon, he was just getting started.

Following his win, however, the people at the World Series of Poker screwed up his name online and listed him on their ranking as Jon Kinkel. Seizing an opportunity, Finkel's friends picked up on the gaff as a new nickname. Finkel took Kinkel in stride. He had been called worse names over the years, of course: Stinkel, Wrinkle, Ronald McFinkel, Finkeltron. It didn't matter what anyone called him anymore. He knew who he was. He was Magic.

JON FINKEL, 1996   **JON FINKEL, 2000**

AFTERWORD

One cold day in November 2005, Jon Finkel boarded a plane for Japan, with his mom, Claire, and his sister, Jenny, by his side. His dad, Mark, had to work, but was there in spirit. Together, they were heading to Yokohama, on Jon's dime, for the 12th Annual Magic: The Gathering World Championship. But this time, Finkel wasn't coming to play. He was coming to be honored.

The occasion was the induction ceremony for the inaugural class of Magic's Pro Tour Hall of Fame. With Magic achieving sport-like status around the world, the makers at Wizards of the Coast felt it was time to give the top players the recognition — and respect — they deserve. When the selection committee cast its ballots for which five players should be in the first class, there was little surprise over who got the most votes. Jonny Magic came out on top again.

For Finkel, it was a fitting cap for this chapter of his life. After years on the outside, he, like his favorite game, had found his groove.

2005 delivered his biggest wins ever. In July, he finished in the money at the main event of the World Series of Poker in Las Vegas, ahead of all his old Magic buddies, including David Williams.

With plenty of cash in the bank, Finkel has begun to reach out beyond the world of gaming to investing. He puts money in real estate, stocks, and a slot machine company. He has also upgraded his lifestyle. After years of sharing tiny apartments with roommates, he decided it was time to branch out on his own. Moving out of his cramped place in the West Village, he took a sprawling 2500 square foot, three bedroom apartment in a stylish enclave of Soho. It's around the corner from his favorite sushi restaurant, where he treats himself to expensive slabs of toro two or three times a week.

With his social life on the rise, he seldom dines alone. Well past his awkward years, and reliance on strategies from Pickupguide.com, Finkel has become confident and competent enough to hold his own. Though his relationship with the Russian model faded, he's meeting plenty of women around town. When he and his friends went to speed dating events, where singles mix and mingle in lightning rounds, Finkel scores the most phone numbers.

One of the consequences of having this book written about him, he says, is that now his dates could know everything about him. "After they read the book, they like me more," he says, "and they want to jump to the girlfriend stage pretty fast." He's still planning to get married and have kids some day, he just hasn't met Mrs. Right yet.

In the meantime, however, he has another gold ring, courtesy of the Magic Hall of Fame. It came during the induction ceremony in Japan. Finkel stood on stage in a natty black suit and crisp red tie. His head was freshly shaved, and two gold hoop earrings hung from his ears. Looking out on the enthusiastic crowd, he smiled nervously as he endured the applause. "All of the players on the stage today support Richard Garfield's claim that Magic the Gathering can be played as an intellectual sport that requires great skill," the announcer said, "Jon Finkel is the closing argument."

Though he hadn't competed in a Magic event since the World's tournament the previous year in San Francisco, he felt a renewed bond with the players. While the rest of his friends, including the all-but-disbanded Lawyers, had given up their other games for poker, Finkel found himself coming full circle. Late at night back in his apartment, he had started up Magic nights with his friends. "It won't be the defining part of my life anymore," he says, "but now that I don't make a living at it anymore, it's a lot of fun to just go back and play Magic."

Upon his induction, Finkel thanked his family and friends, and, later, gave a special shout-out to his father. "The reason I was able to become the best Magic player in the world was clearly my Dad," he said, "He bought me my first computer in 1981 and played games with me my whole life."

At the end of the event, Richard Garfield happily sealed the deal by presenting him with a Hall of Fame ring. The solid gold band is encrusted with five jewels representing each color of Magic cards. On one side is his name. Not Jonny Magic or Finkeltron. Just Finkel.

February 2006

APPENDIX A
Magic: The Gathering Basics

Magic: The Gathering is a deeply complex game that can be played on a variety of levels. Its rules deserve a detailed and comprehensive explanation.

This isn't one of them.

This appendix is an abridged and editorialized version of the rules meant to help Magic newbies through my book. To explain the complete rules would require a sixty-three-page book unto itself. And, thankfully, someone's already written that one. It comes with an introductory set of Magic cards, readily available wherever life-altering games are sold. Players can also get their feet wet via Magic Online (www.magicthegathering.com). For those still feeling stuck, hunt down the nearest hobby shop and wander inside. Maybe the next Jonny Magic will be there, ready to take you under his—or her—wing.

THE GAME

Magic: The Gathering is a card game. To play, each competitor needs a deck of Magic cards; you can either construct your own deck of cards, or use a prepackaged set. You'll also need paper and pencil to keep track of the scores.

THE OBJECT

Each player starts the game with 20 points. You win when you cut the other player's score down to 0, or when your opponent has no more cards to draw. If both players drop simultaneously to 0, the game is a tie.

TYPES OF CARDS

There are several types of Magic cards, but they fall under two basic categories: lands and spells.

Spells Spells are the cards you use to combat your opponent. They have comic book–style names like Tangle Golem (a gruesome creature) or Spawning Pit (a magical artifact). Each spell has its own ability. Some make your opponent do something undesirable, like sacrifice a certain number of cards from his deck. Others are used to attack or defend; these cards show corresponding numeric values. When you attack, the spell takes away a designated number of points from your opponent; when you defend, it blocks against a certain number of points.

A Tangle Golem, for example, has an offensive power of 5 points and defensive toughness of 4. This means that in combat, it can deal 5 points of damage to the opposing creature or player but will withstand only 4 points of damage.

But to cast a spell, you need lands (see below).

Lands Lands are the cards you need in order to use spells. Each spell has its respective cost written at the top of the card. For example, a spell called Infested Roothold costs 4 lands to play. (If you want to get geeky about it, picture yourself as a wizard on a mountain-top, sucking up rays of power from the land beneath you into the palms of your hands. In Magic's mythology, you use the lands to make "mana," the magic power that unleashes your spells.) Land cards come in the form of Swamps, Mountains, Islands, Plains, and Forests.

THE PLAY

A coin flip decides who goes first. Each player then shuffles his deck and draws seven cards. If you don't like your cards, you can shuffle them back into your deck. But each time you redraw, you have to take one less card.

You begin by drawing a card from the top of your deck. You then place one of your land cards faceup on the table in front of you; only one land can be put into play each turn. To use a land, you turn it sideways; this is called "tapping" the card. Once tapped, you can lay down a corresponding spell (sometimes you might need to tap a number of lands before having enough to use a spell) to combat the other player.

Your opponent then goes through the same steps on his turn: drawing, tapping, and doing whatever he can to keep his score high, and make yours low. At the beginning of each turn, you twist your tapped sideways cards back up—this is called "untapping" your cards—and begin again. Discards go into a pile called, appropriately, the graveyard.

Sample Round of Play A sample round of play may look like this:

Jack: Draws a card from his deck, and places a Forest land card on the table. He taps the Forest by turning it sideways, then puts a Willow Elf, which requires 1 Forest land, in front of it.

Jill: Draws a card, and puts a Forest land on the table.

Jack: Untaps his Forest, and draws another card. Plays a Plains card by placing it next to his Forest. Jack taps his Willow Elf, turning it sideways, to attack. The Willow Elf has an attack strength of 1, as written on the bottom corner of the card. Jill loses 1 point. The score is now Jack 20, Jill 19.

MAGIC TOURNAMENTS

The vast majority of Magic games take place in homes, dorms, pizza shops, backseats, bars, high school bathrooms, Fortune 500 conference rooms, and anywhere else there's a flat surface.

Eventually, some players like to try their skills in tournaments. There are thousands of Magic tournaments held every week around the world. In order to compete at a Pro Tour competition, players must first qualify at local events (known as meatgrinders). Once on the Pro Tour, players accumulate points based on how they finish. These points are used to calculate standings and qualifications to compete at the National and World championships.

Tournament Formats There are two basic formats for tournament play: Limited and Constructed.

In Constructed play, competitors assemble and bring their own decks to the event.

In Limited events, players receive the same packs of sealed Magic cards, and must use these to make their decks. There are two types of Limited play: Drafts and Sealed Decks. For Drafts, players sit around a table and take turns selecting cards from a communal pool. In Sealed play, competitors just rip open their packs and compete.

MORE INFO

For more on Magic rules, news, and tournaments, go to their Web site: magicthegathering.com.

APPENDIX B

Texas Hold 'Em
Poker Basics

Poker, like Magic: The Gathering, is a game of art and science, luck and skill. It is relatively simple to learn but difficult to master. Because a variation known as Texas Hold 'Em epitomizes these qualities (and has plenty of betting), it has become, in the words of poker legend Doyle Brunson, the "Cadillac" of the game.

It's also the way most of the players in *Jonny Magic and the Card Shark Kids* prefer to ride. For this reason, I'm limiting this appendix to a basic explanation of Texas Hold 'Em's two primary formats—limit and no limit. For those new to the game, I'm also including the standard poker hand rankings.

RANK OF HANDS (BEST TO WORST)
Note: There is no ranking of the suits—diamonds, hearts, spades, clubs.

Royal Flush Ten, Jack, Queen, King, Ace, all of the same suit.

Straight Flush A sequence of five cards of the same suit. Between two straight flushes, the one with the higher top card wins. For example, 3-4-5-6-7 of hearts beats 2-3-4-5-6 of spades (since an Ace can be played low, however, a straight flush of 2-3-4-5-6 beats A-2-3-4-5).

Four of a Kind Four cards of the same rank.

Full House Three cards of one rank, two of another—for example, three Jacks and two 10s.

Flush Five cards of the same suit, but out of sequence, such as 2-4-7-10-Q of diamonds.

Straight Five cards in a sequence, but different suits.

Three of a Kind Any three cards of the same rank.

Two Pair Two cards of one rank, two of another. Between two players holding two pairs, the player with the higher pair wins (for example, 10-10-5-5-9 beats 9-9-8-8-6). When the high pairs are the same, the player with the higher low pair wins (so 6-6-4-4-10 beats 6-6-2-2-3). If the high and low pairs are identical, then the higher remaining card wins; J-J-7-7-8 is better than J-J-7-7-5.

Pair Two cards of identical rank.

High Card When no player holds any of the hands listed above, the person with the highest card wins. If competing players hold the same high card, then the next highest card is compared, and so on.

TEXAS HOLD 'EM RULES

Object To make the best possible poker hand using five cards.

The Cards A standard fifty-two-card deck.

Limit vs. No Limit There are two main types of Texas Hold 'Em play: Limit and No Limit.

In Limit play, the casinos or players determine two sizes of minimum bets that are made at different points in the game. In a $100/$200 game, for example, all bets and raises must be in $100 increments during the first two rounds of play; bets are in $200 increments during the last two.

No Limit play has the added drama of allowing a player to push in all of her chips at any moment and declare "all-in."

The Dealer In lieu of a casino dealer, each player takes turns distributing the cards. A small marker called a "dealer button" moves clockwise around the table after each round of play, designating the deal.

STEPS OF PLAY

The Blinds Before the cards are dealt, two mandatory bets start the game. These are called "the blinds" because they're made before the bettors see their cards. The player to the immediate left of the dealer bets first, posting half of the minimum bet; this is called the "small blind" (in a $100/$200 game, the small blind equals $50). The player to the small blind's left posts the next bet, called the "big blind" (equivalent to the full minimum bet or, in this example, $100).

The Deal The dealer distributes one card facedown to each player, moving clockwise around the table, and repeats until each player holds two cards (called the "hole" cards).

Bets The player to the left of the big blind makes the first bet. The minimum bet is equal to the big blind (in our example, $100). If the player doesn't like his hand, he can fold. Each subsequent player then makes one of three types of bets. He can relinquish or "fold" his hand, match the bet of the person before him (to "call"), or raise the bet.

The Flop The dealer discards, or "burns," the top card of the deck (an old ploy to dupe cheaters), then deals three cards faceup in the middle of the table. These communal cards are called "the flop."

Bets The person to the left of the dealer makes the first play; he now has the additional option to "check," which allows him to stay in the game without now tossing in chips. If he checks, the next player has the same four options, and so on. Once a player raises, however, the others must at least call to stay in.

The Turn The dealer now burns one card, and places another faceup on the table next to the flop. This card is called "the turn" or "fourth street."

Bets Another round of betting occurs.

The River The dealer burns one, then deals the fifth and final communal card, called "the river" or "fifth street."

Bets The last round of betting follows.

APPENDIX C
Blackjack Basics

CARDS

Blackjack is played using one or a combination of standard fifty-two-card decks. Casinos often deal a number of shuffled decks, up to eight at a time, from a dispenser called a "shoe."

OBJECT

To outscore the dealer's hand, without going over 21 points.

POINTS

Points are scored according to the numeric value of each card. Face cards are worth 10, and an Ace counts for either 1 or 11, depending on the player's choice. All other card values correspond to their number.

OPENING BETS

Players bet before cards are dealt.

THE DEAL

The dealer deals one card at a time to each player, starting with the player on his left. Each player gets two cards faceup. The dealer deals himself two cards as well—the first one facedown, the second, known as the up card, faceup.

BLACKJACK

If the player or dealer gets an Ace and a face or 10 card, that makes 21, or blackjack; players who nail a blackjack are paid at a rate of 3-to-2 on their bet, unless the dealer has blackjack, too. If the dealer is showing an Ace up card, some casinos allow the player to take a side bet called "insurance": a bet, half the amount of the player's original wager, that the dealer does in fact have 21. If the dealer hits blackjack, the player receives a 2-to-1.

If both the player and dealer have 21, this is called a "push," which means the player hangs on to the opening bet. If neither the dealer nor the player has blackjack in the opening hand, then the player has four options for what to do next: hit, stand, double-down, or split.

Hit To request another card and try to score closer to 21, a player "hits." This is signaled by either tapping or scratching the felt. A player can hit until she reaches or surpasses 21 points.

Stand When not wanting more cards, a player "stands" by waving her hand facedown over the cards.

Double-down If a player thinks she can reach or get close to 21 with just one card, she can double-down, which means making an additional bet equal to her original one, for which she'll receive one final card.

Split In a case when her initial two cards have the same value, she can request to split them and play each hand separately. A player who exceeds 21 points at any time busts, and loses her bet.

THE DEALER'S HAND

After the players complete their hands, the dealer reveals his facedown card. If he doesn't have blackjack or a total of 17 points, he must hit until he scores at least 17. If he beats the player's score, the player loses his bet. If he ties, it's a push. If he busts, the player gets paid back at a rate of 1-to-1.

BASIC STRATEGY

Next to card counting, so-called basic strategy is considered the optimal way of playing blackjack. Without playing basic strategy, a player is at roughly a 2 to 3 percent disadvantage to the dealer; with it, the player's disadvantage decreases to about 0.5 percent. Basic strategy depends on how many decks are in play. However, a standard chart based on multiple decks is provided below (S = Stand; H = Hit; D = Double-down; Sp = Split). In addition, there's one general rule: never take insurance.

PLAYER'S HAND	DEALER'S HAND									
	2	3	4	5	6	7	8	9	10	A
8	H	H	H	H	H	H	H	H	H	H
9	H	D	D	D	D	H	H	H	H	H
10	D	D	D	D	D	D	D	D	H	H
11	D	D	D	D	D	D	D	D	D	H
12	H	H	S	S	S	H	H	H	H	H
13	S	S	S	S	S	H	H	H	H	H
14	S	S	S	S	S	H	H	H	H	H
15	S	S	S	S	S	H	H	H	H	H
16	S	S	S	S	S	H	H	H	H	H
17	S	S	S	S	S	S	S	S	S	S
A,2	H	H	H	D	D	H	H	H	H	H
A,3	H	H	H	D	D	H	H	H	H	H
A,4	H	H	D	D	D	H	H	H	H	H
A,5	H	H	D	D	D	H	H	H	H	H
A,6	H	D	D	D	D	H	H	H	H	H
A,7	S	D	D	D	D	S	S	H	H	H

A,8	S	S	S	S	S	S	S	S	S	S
A,9	S	S	S	S	S	S	S	S	S	S
A,A	SP	SP	SP	SP	SP	SP	SP	SP	SP	SP
2,2	H	H	SP	SP	SP	SP	H	H	H	H
3,3	H	H	SP	SP	SP	SP	H	H	H	H
4,4	H	H	H	H	H	H	H	H	H	H
5,5	D	D	D	D	D	D	D	D	H	H
6,6	H	SP	SP	SP	SP	H	H	H	H	H
7,7	SP	SP	SP	SP	SP	SP	H	H	H	H
8,8	SP	SP	SP	SP	SP	SP	SP	SP	SP	SP
9,9	SP	SP	SP	SP	SP	S	SP	SP	S	S
10,10	S	S	S	S	S	S	S	S	S	S

CARD COUNTING

In blackjack, a player's odds of winning improve when there's a greater concentration of Aces and 10s remaining in the shoe. This is true for two reasons: it increases both the likelihood of hitting blackjack and the chances that the dealer, who must hit until he reaches at least 17, will bust.

Card counting allows players to keep track of the cards that have been dealt in order to determine when there's a greater concentration of high cards (10s through Aces) remaining. "Card counting," however, is something of a misnomer. Players don't literally count, say, every Queen that's dealt. Instead, they assign a value to the sets of high and low cards. This is considered the "Hi-Lo Count":

10, J, Q, K, A: −1
2, 3, 4, 5, 6: +1
7, 8, 9: 0

Throughout play, the card counter keeps what's known as a "running count," adding and subtracting as each card hits the table. For example:

A dealer deals a Jack (card value −1); the count is −1.

Next card is a 3 (value +1); +1 plus −1 (the prior running count) = 0.

Next card, 4 (value +1); + 1 plus 0 (prior running count) = +1.

Next, 2 (value +1); count becomes +2.

And so on . . .

When the count gets positive, that means there are more 10s and Aces remaining in the deck, thus spiking up the odds for a high hand or blackjack. For greater precision, a so-called true count is determined by dividing the running count by the approximate number of decks remaining. So if the running count is, say, +10, and there are roughly two decks remaining in the shoe, the true count equals +5 (10 divided by 2).

Counters like to have a true count of at least +2 or higher before betting big. The idea is to bet less when the count is negative, and more when it's positive. During a positive count, the player's advantage can rise as high as 5 percent—small, but significant.

UNDERSTANDING THE ODDS

Blackjack may be beatable, but it's not necessarily a winning game. Even players employing perfect basic strategy are likely to lose in the long run. Card counters sometimes experience massive swings, since the edge is so slight. To win in the long run requires a sizable bankroll to ride out the tide, plus a healthy dose of brains, teamwork, and guts. In short, there's a reason very few people succeed.

GLOSSARY

When specified: M = Magic, P = Poker, B = Blackjack

Action Bets, the bigger the better. (P)

All-in To bet all of one's chips. (P)

Ante A mandatory bet made prior to the deal.

Artifact A type of spell card, signifying a magical object. (M)

Attack To deal damage against an opponent in an effort to reduce his score. (M)

Back counting Counting cards while watching, not playing, at a table. (B)

Bankroll The money used to finance a period of betting.

Basic strategy A system for optimizing blackjack play. (B)

Bet A voluntary wager.

Bet spread The variation between a player's maximum and minimum wagers. (B)

Big blind A forced bet, equal to the minimum wager in a game, made before the deal by the person two seats to the left of the dealer. (P)

Big Player The person on a blackjack team who places the bet at the table. (B)

BJ Abbreviation for blackjack. (B)

Black One of the five colors of Magic cards. Black cards invoke death and disease, monsters from black lagoons, and tarlike poisons. (M)

Blackjack Hitting a score of 21 points using only the first two cards dealt. (B)

Blank A card that does not improve a player's hand. (P)

Blinds The forced bets made by the two players to the dealer's left prior to the deal. They include the small blind (half the minimum bet) and the big blind (the full minimum bet). (P)

Block To use a card to counter an opponent's attack. (M)

Blue One of the five colors of Magic cards. Blue draws magic of the sea and sky. (M)

Bluff To bet or raise with a hand that's likely not the best.

Board The community cards dealt faceup on the table. This includes the flop, turn, and river. (P)

Booster pack A supplementary package of fifteen random Magic cards, used to expand one's collection. (M)

BP Abbreviation for Big Player. (B)

Burn To discard the top card of a deck before dealing in an effort to prevent cheating. (P)

Bust Exceeding 21 points in blackjack. (B)

Button A small disc used to represent the dealer. (P)

Buy-in The amount of money required to enter a game. For example, the main event of the World Series of Poker requires a $10,000 buy-in. (P)

Cage The cashier area of a casino.

Call To match a prior bet. (P)

Check To abstain from betting, but retain the right to wager later in the round. (P)

Check-raise To check, and then raise in the same round of betting. (P)

Chip Disc used to represent a unit of money.

Combat To attack, defend, or block using cards in play. (M)

Construct To assemble a deck from a pool of cards. (M)

Controller A member of a blackjack team who keeps a running count of the cards and signals a Big Player when and how to bet. (B)

Counting BP A Big Player able to keep his own running count and use it effectively. (B)

Creature A Magic card representing a fighting animal, human, or beast. (M)

Cut card A plastic card, often yellow, used to cut a portion of cards in a combination of decks. (B)

Damage The amount of lost points inflicted during an attack. (M)

Deck The collected cards used to play Magic. There is a forty-card minimum for limited play and a sixty-card minimum for constructed. (M)

Deuce A 2 card.

Double-down A blackjack play in which the bettor doubles his bet but receives only one additional card. (B)

Draft A form of tournament play in which players take turns selecting cards to include in their decks from a communal pool. (M)

Draw (Magic) To select the top card from a player's library. (M)

Draw (poker) When a player can make a flush or a straight using one or two unrevealed cards on the board. (P)

Edge A percentage of advantage according to the odds.

Enchantment A type of spell card. (M)

EV Abbreviation for "expected value." (B)

Expected value The amount a player can expect to win or lose on a given bet. (B)

Fifth street The first community card dealt on the board; also known as the river. (P)

Fish A weak player; also known as a sucker.

Flavor The descriptive text that appears on a Magic card. (M)

Flop The first three community cards shown simultaneously faceup. (P)

Flush Five cards of the same suit. (P)

Fold To discard a hand.

Forests One of the five types of land cards, colored green. (M)

Fourth street The fourth community card, also called the turn. (P)

Freeroll A situation in which a player can only win money, not lose it.

Full house Two cards of one rank, three of another. (P)

Gorilla BP A Big Player who does not keep a running count. (B)

Graveyard A pile for discarded cards accumulated during play. (M)

Green One of the five colors of cards. Corresponds to spells and monsters of the earth, such as man-eating worms and thorn-covered spirits. (M)

Griffin Book The database of suspected card counters and casino cheats maintained by the Griffin Investigations detective agency.

Heads-up Two players competing against each other.

Heat The level of suspicion on a card counter.

Hi-Lo Count A method of counting cards. (B)

Hit To request an additional card, signaled by tapping or scratching the felt by a player's cards. (B)

Hold 'Em A variation of poker in which players must make the best possible hand using at least one hole card and any combination of the five faceup community cards. (P)

Hole cards The cards dealt facedown to a player.

Instant A type of spell card. (M)

Insurance The option to place a side bet, equivalent to half a player's original bet, to protect against the dealer hitting blackjack. (B)

Interrupt A type of spell card. (M)

Island One of five types of land cards, colored blue. (M)

Land Resource cards used to cast spells; land types include Forests, Swamps, Islands, Mountains, and Plains. (M)

Library The pile of cards from which a player draws. (M)

Life The total number of a player's points. Each player starts with 20 points. A player whose score drops to 0 loses. (M)

Limp To make the minimum bet. (P)

Loose A player who bets often and plays many hands. (P)

Mana The energy, created by using land cards, and used to cast spells. (M)

Mana pool The amount of Mana a player has at a given moment. (M)

Mountain One of the five types of land cards, colored red. (M)

M:tG Abbreviation for Magic: The Gathering. (M)

Muck To discard a hand.

No Limit A game in which players can push in all their chips at any point. (P)

Nuts The best possible hand. (P)

Off-suit Hole cards of different suits. (P)

Outs The possible cards that enable a player to win a hand. (P)

Penetration The approximate number of decks being dealt from a shoe, after cut with the cut card. Once the cut card is reached, for example, the shoe is reshuffled. (B)

Pit The area of blackjack tables in a casino. (B)

Pit boss The casino employee in charge of supervising the pit. (B)

Plains One of the five types of land cards, colored white. (M)

Position A player's place at the table in relation to that of the dealer's. (P)

Post To put a blind or ante into the pot before the deal. (P)

Pot The money, gathered in the middle of the table, that is at stake in a game. (P)

Power The designated damage dealt by a creature card, printed numerically on the card's bottom right corner on the left side of the slash mark. (M)

Rail The dividing line between spectators and players.

Raise To meet and increase the size of a bet by no less than the same size. (P)

Rake The percentage of a pot taken by a casino or online site.

Read To analyze another player's behavior in the effort to discern that player's hand.

Red One of the five colors of Magic cards; red conjures the fiercest and most ferocious creatures and enchantments—fire-breathing dragons, hellacious goblins. (M)

Reraise To raise after another person has already raised. (P)

River The last community card dealt faceup on the board. (P)

Rock A tight player, who plays conservatively and bets mainly with very good hands. (P)

Running count The total number of points accumulated while tracking cards using the Hi-Lo Count. (B)

Sacrifice To put a card into one's graveyard. (M)

Set Three cards of the same rank. (P)

Shoe The device that contains one or more decks of cards dealt in blackjack. (B)

Shuffle tracking An advanced method of card counting in which a player assigns a count to a chunk of cards in a shoe and follows those chunks through the shuffle. (B)

Small blind The forced bet made by the player to the left of the dealer, half the size of the big blind or minimum bet. (P)

Sorcery A type of spell card. (M)

Spells Type of Magic cards used to combat an opponent. (M)

Spotter A member of a blackjack team who tracks the running count, and signals when the count becomes positive. (B)

Stand To cease drawing cards, signaled by waving a hand over the table.

Suited Cards of the same suit. (P)

Swamp One of the five types of land card, colored black. (M)

Tap To put a Magic card into play by turning it sideways. (M)

Target The player or card chosen for a spell to affect. (M)

Tell An unconscious tic that may reveal a player's hand.

Tight To play conservatively. (P)

Tilt To get angry and negative while playing badly and, thus, do worse. (P)

Toughness The designated defensive value of a card, printed numerically on the card's bottom right corner on the right side of the slash mark. (M)

True Count The running count divided by the approximate number of decks remaining to be dealt. (B)

Under the gun The first player to bet. (P)

Unit A predesignated betting amount.

Untap The first step in a phase of Magic play, in which any and all tapped cards are turned back to their original position and, essentially, disengaged. (M)

Up Card The dealer's first card, which is dealt faceup. (B)

White One of the five colors of Magic cards. White conjures lawful clerics and angels. (M)

Wizards of the Coast Publisher and developer of Magic: The Gathering.

WotC Abbreviation for Wizards of the Coast.

NOTES

PRELUDE: THE NEW HIGH ROLLERS

xii   "army of amateurs": "Not in the Cards," *Slate*, June 4, 2004,
     http://slate.msn.com/id/2101781.

xii   "year of the young guns": "Tournament Report: Event Number 13, No Limit
     Hold 'Em," *Poker Pages*, May 4, 2004, www.pokerpages.com/tournament/
     results8722.htm.

xiv "cardboard crack": "Cardboard Crack," *Commonwealth Appeal*, March 9, 1996,
     p. 1C.

3. THE MAGIC BULLET

28   "Generation Hex": "Generation Hex," *People*, March 13, 1995, p. 72.

28   in Madison, Wisconsin: "Magic Cards," *Wisconsin State Journal*, September 21,
     1995, p. 3.

28   schools banned it: "Players Can Spend Thousands on Card Games,"
     San Francisco Chronicle, February 24, 1995, p. A1.

28   "The Devil . . . is settling in": "A Parents Group in Pound Ridge Wrestles the
     Devil for Halloween," *New York Times*, October 31, 1995, p. B5.

29   *Brandweek* magazine dubbed: "The Most Intriguing Marketers of 1996,"
     Brandweek, November 13, 1995, p. 46.

29   In Sacramento, California: "It's Magic," *The Advocate,* January 13, 1995, p. 19.

4. JERSEY KIDS VS. DEAD GUYS

45   "Cheaters should be publicly humiliated . . .": "The C.H.E.A.T. List,"
     April 14, 1998, http://www.classicdojo.org/b982/bo.980414hlo.txt.

45   "Jon Finkel decided . . .": "Enter the Fungosaur," *Play or Draw,* date n/a,
     http://www.playordraw.com/db/print.asp?ID=20.

47   Taking home a $10,000 third-place prize: Pro Tour Chicago 1997 Results,
     http://www.wizards.com/sideboard/article.asp?x=results/PTCHICAGO98.

47   He wished he had a dad: "Is This Man the Future of Poker?" *Playboy,* January
     2005, p. 187.

48   $25,000 going: Pro Tour New York, 1998, http://www.wizards.com/
     sideboard/article.asp?x=results/PTNY98.

51   "only brings a smile": "PTNY Tourney Report Rap," April 22, 1998,
     http://misetings.com/item/507.

5. FINKELTRON

59   "giggling, unshaven madman": "Quarterfinals: Zvi Mowshowitz vs. Keith
     McLaughlin," StarCityGames, http://www.starcitygames.com/php/news/
     article/5693.html.

6. ROUNDERS

73   "the most fascinating of all the various forms": Doyle Brunson, with Bobby
     Baldwin, Mike Caro, Joey Hawthorne, Chip Reese, and David Sklansky,
     Super/System: A Course in Power Poker (Las Vegas: B&G, 1978), p. 331.

76   "the games of a people": Marshall McLuhan, *Understand Media: The Extensions
     of Man* (New York: McGraw-Hill, 1964), pp. 209–210.

83   Pumping a $20 million publicity campaign: "Mania for 'Pocket Monsters'
     Yields Billions for Nintendo," *New York Times,* April 26, 1999, p. A1.

83   they sent a fleet: Ibid.

83   one thousand stuffed Pokemon dolls: Ibid.

83   four thousand kids: Ibid.

84   A nine-year-old in Long Island: "Beware of the Poke Mania," *Time,* November 22, 1999, p. 80.

84   A six-year-old got busted: Ibid.

84   "Grownups aren't ready": Ibid.

84   sales of Pokemon cards approached $1 billion: Ibid.

85   "Don't kid yourself": "MTG a Better Game Than Poker and Chess?"
     rec.games.chess.misc, July 22, 2001.

7. JONNY MAGIC

97 "As I picked up my winnings": Edward O. Thorp, *Beat the Dealer: A Winning Strategy for the Game of Twenty-One* (New York: Vintage Books, 1966), p. 64.

101 Lawyers: To retain their anonymity, the Lawyers team nickname, as well as the names of cofounders Sylvia and Vinny and members Dan, Don, Angela, Stew, and Gems, was changed; they are the only pseudonyms in this book.

9. SEND IN THE CLOWNS

137 "Before . . . the specter of Jon Finkel": "Pro-Tour New Orleans Wrap-Up," http://www.wizards.com/sideboard/article.asp?x=PTNOR01\500recap.

138 "Sometimes Jon doesn't care": "House of Cards," *New City Chicago,* January 22, 2003, http://www.newcitychicago.com/chicago/2205.html.

138 "They'd better hurry up": "Semi-Finals: Kai Budde vs. Jon Finkel," http://www.wizards.com/default.asp?x=sideboard/ptchi03/sf2.

139 "Magic King Loses His Crown": "House of Cards," Ibid.

146 Bonanza: "Father's Day Bonanza," *Blackjack Insider Newsletter* 42, July 2003, www.blackjackinsider.com/newsletter_42.

10. ALL-IN

152 "Poker is a stylish mix of strategy": "The World Poker Tour Is TV's Newest" (press release), August 1, 2003.

154 "more money than I had a right to even dream about": Chris Moneymaker, with Daniel Paisner, *Moneymaker: How an Amateur Poker Player Turned $40 into $2.5 Million at the World Series of Poker* (New York: Harper Collins, 2005), p. 209.

154 The sun was coming up: My story of Jordan Berkowitz originally appeared in different form in an article I wrote for *Sync* magazine. "America's Greatest Online Poker Player," *Sync,* December/January 2005, pp. 112–115.

11. THE FINAL TABLE

160 "the biggest game this world has to offer": James McManus, *Positively Fifth Street: Murders, Cheetahs, and Binion's World Series of Poker* (New York: Farrar, Straus, and Giroux, 2003), p. 47.

161 "If it's true, this is a great story": "Beware a Sheep in Wolf's Clothing," *Poker Pages,* May 2002, http://www.pokerpages.com/tournament/result5281.htm.

161 "Pikula probably forgot to mention": "Chris Pikula Makes Final Table at WSOP Shootout," May 20, 2002, http://www.misetings.com/item/473.

168 "The Internet is a great teaching tool": "Tournament Report: Event Number 13, No Limit Hold 'Em," *Poker Pages,* May 4, 2004, www.pokerpages.com/tournament/results8722.htm.

169 "Is there something": Subject: David Williams, rec.gambling.poker, May 27, 2004.

169 "My son plays MTG": Ibid.

169 "A lot of the new faces": Ibid., May 29, 2004.

12. THE ONLY GAME IN TOWN

175 "chilling and bluffing their way": "Poker at an Early Age; Not Just Another Teen Fad," *USA Today,* December 20, 2004, Life section, p. 1A.

175 "Do you know where": "Poker Faces, and They Haven't Started Shaving," *New York Times,* October 31, 2004, p. 1.

175 "It's bad enough that the federal government": "For Teenagers, This Gamble Isn't Worth It," *Newsday,* December 7, 2004, http://www.newsday.com/news/columnists/ny-paulvitello,0,6580338.columnist?coll=ny-news-columnists.

EPILOGUE

180 "Poker themes are great": "Count 'Em In: Local Groups Eye Poker's Popularity for Fund-Raisers," *Andover Townsman,* January 27, 2005, http://www.andovertownsman.com/news/archive.html.

180 "Poker was always": "Young Guns Come Out Firing," *Poker Pages,* December 30, 2004, http://www.pokerpages.com/blog/index.php?itemid=84.

180 "the future of poker": "Is This Man the Future of Poker?" *Playboy,* January 2005, p. 9.

BIBLIOGRAPHY

BOOKS

Alvarez, A. *The Biggest Game in Town.* New York: Houghton Mifflin, 1983.

Anderson, Ian. *Turning the Tables on Las Vegas: How to Win at Blackjack, Poker and Life's Games.* New York: Vintage, 1976.

Asbury, Herbert. *Sucker's Progress: An Informal History of Gambling in America.* New York: Dodd, Mead, and Company, 1938.

Bellin, Andy. *Poker Nation: A High-Stakes, Low-Life Adventure into the Heart of a Gambling Country.* New York: Perennial, 2002.

Brunson, Doyle, with Bobby Baldwin, Mike Caro, Joey Hawthorne, Chip Reese, and David Sklansky. *Super/System: A Course in Power Poker.* Las Vegas: B&G, 1978.

Card, Orson Scott. *Ender's Game.* New York: Tor, 1985.

Denton, Sally, and Roger Morris. *The Money and the Power: The Making of Las Vegas and Its Hold on America, 1947–2000.* New York: Knopf, 2001.

Dostoevsky, Fyodor. *The Gambler.* Translated by Pevear and Volokhonsky. New York: Knopf, 1993.

Dungeon Master Guide: Advanced Dungeons and Dragons. Renton, Wash.: TSR, 1995.

Gygax, Gary. *Master of the Game: Principles and Techniques for Becoming an Expert Role-Playing Game Master.* New York: Perigee Books, 1989.

————. *Role-Playing Mastery: Tips, Tactics and Strategies for Improving Your Participation in Any Role-Playing Game—By One of the People Who Started It All.* New York: Perigee Books, 1989.

Holden, Anthony. *Big Deal: A Year as Professional Poker Player.* Toronto: McClelland & Stewart, 1990.

Kaplan, Michael, and Brad Reagan. *Aces and Kings: Inside Stories and Million-Dollar Strategies from Poker's Greatest Players.* New York: Wenner Books, 2005.

Konik, Michael. *The Man with the $100,000 Breasts and Other Gambling Stories.* Las Vegas: Huntington Press, 1997.

McDonald, Glenn. *Deal Me In! Online Cardrooms, Big-Time Tournaments, and the New Poker.* Alameda, Calif.: Sybex, 2005.

McLuhan, Marshall. *Understand Media: The Extensions of Man.* New York: McGraw-Hill, 1964.

McManus, James. *Positively Fifth Street: Murders, Cheetahs, and Binion's World Series of Poker.* New York: Farrar, Straus and Giroux, 2003.

Mezrich, Ben. *Bringing Down the House: The Inside Story of Six M.I.T. Students Who Took Vegas for Millions.* New York: Free Press, 2002.

Miller, G. Wayne. *Toy Wars: The Epic Struggle Between G.I. Joe, Barbie, and the Companies That Make Them.* New York: Times Books, 1998.

Moneymaker, Chris, with Daniel Paisner. *Moneymaker: How an Amateur Poker Player Turned $40 into $2.5 Million at the World Series of Poker.* New York: HarperCollins, 2005.

Moursund, Beth, and Cory J. Herndon, Brian Tinsman, Jeff Jordan, Joseph DeVincentis Jr., and Mark Rosewater. *The Complete Encyclopedia of Magic: The Gathering.* New York: Thunder's Mouth Press, 2002.

Sklansky, David. *Hold'Em Poker.* Henderson, Nev.: Two Plus Two, 1997.

Sklansky, David, and Mason Malmuth. *Hold'Em Poker for Advanced Players.* Henderson, Nev.: Two Plus Two, 1999.

Swain, James. *Funny Money.* New York: Ballantine Books, 2002.

30 Years of Adventure: A Celebration of Dungeons and Dragons. Renton, Wash.: Wizards of the Coast, 2004.

Thompson, Hunter S. *Fear and Loathing in Las Vegas.* New York: Random House, 1971.

Thorp, Edward O. *Beat the Dealer: A Winning Strategy for the Game of Twenty-One.* New York: Vintage Books, 1966.

Uston, Ken. *The Big Player: How a Team of Blackjack Players Made a Million Dollars.* New York: Holt, Rinehart, and Winston, 1977.

————. *Ken Uston on Blackjack: Secrets of Winning at '21' by the $5,000,000 Man.* Fort Lee, N.J.: Barricade Books, 1986.

Williams, Pete. *Card Sharks: How Upper Deck Turned a Child's Hobby into a High-Stakes, Billion-Dollar Business.* New York: MacMillan, 1995.

ONLINE

Wizards of the Coast: www.wizards.com

Magic: The Gathering: www.magicthegathering.com

Star City Games: www.starcitygames.com—Magic strategy

Brainburst: www.brainburst.com—Magic strategy

Cardplayer: www.cardplayer.com—poker magazine

Classic Dojo: www.classicdojo.org/—Magic archives

rec.games.trading-cards.magic.misc—Magic newsgroup

rec.games.trading-cards.magic.strategy—Magic strategy newsgroup

Party Poker: www.partypoker.com—online gambling

Poker Stars: www.pokerstars.com—online gambling

Paradise Poker: www.paradisepoker.com—online gambling

Poker Pages: www.pokerpages.com

Rec.gambling.poker—poker newsgroup

Two Plus Two: www.twoplustwo.com/—poker strategy

Stanford Wong's BJ21: www.bj21.com/—blackjack strategy

Griffin Investigations: www.griffininvestigations.com

World Series of Poker: www.worldseriesofpoker.com

World Poker Tour: www.worldpokertour.com

AUTHOR'S NOTE

Like a lot of guys in their thirties (or at least those willing to admit it), I'm one of the freaks and geeks who grew up on comic books, Tolkien novels, and Dungeons and Dragons. I knew I wanted to write a book set in this world. I was curious about how fantasy, and fantasy games, can transform someone's life for real. The question was: whose story to tell? The answer, like a round of D&D, would put me on an unexpected adventure of my own.

After a few false starts, my quest kept leading back to Magic. I had long been interested in the game, which initially seemed like D&D for the next generation. But, in fact, Magic isn't much of a fantasy game after all. Though it shares the iconography of wizards and warriors, it's more strategic and competitive. Still, it attracts the sort of obsessive players who turn their lives over to a game. I wondered if there was one out of the millions who had been most transformed. When I phoned Richard Garfield, the creator of Magic, to see if he knew any potential candidates, he didn't skip a beat. "Yes," he said, "Jon Finkel."

Finkel had been World Champ at Magic, but beyond that remained something of a mystery. Early pictures online showed this awkward pudgy teen with Kool-Aid-colored hair and thick glasses; more recent ones revealed a slim confident city kid with hoop earrings, a backward baseball cap, and a goatee. Though he still showed up at Magic tournaments, the collective opinion in the community was that Finkel's mind was elsewhere. When I reached him by phone at his apartment in New York, he told me where he'd been. "I've been playing some poker," he said, "and I was on this card-counting team for a while. Now I'm betting sports."

A few days later, I was sitting outside at the White Horse Tavern in the Village, having what would be the first of dozens of interviews with Jonny Magic. Over the next year, I followed him from game shops to sushi bars, Magic tournaments to poker rooms, Seattle to Atlantic City. Along the way, I met and interviewed dozens of other card shark kids. I watched Finkel bet thousands on golf, play Hold 'Em at Harrah's, and kick cigarettes in New York. We clocked so many hours talking in diners that, at least once, we got asked to leave.

To get behind the scenes of Magic's creation, I spent many long afternoons with Garfield in his game-strewn office, breaking for the occasional Starbucks refueling or round of cards with his family. I tracked down all the other key players at Wizards of the Coast, going to their Seattle headquarters and digging through their vast archives of magazines, games, Web coverage, and videos. I trolled gaming conventions, and made pilgrimages to Florida and Wisconsin, respectively, to meet with the cocreators of D&D, Dave Arneson and Gary Gygax.

To better understand and appreciate Finkel's experience in the gambling world, I enrolled in my own independent study course in poker and blackjack. I read books and sites on strategy and history, and watched hours of poker tournament reruns while working out on the elliptical machine. Though I'd played in poker nights for years, I sharpened my game online and enrolled in a World Poker

Tour boot camp in Vegas, taught by Mike Sexton, host of the popular show. Yeah, I lost.

During one of many other trips to Vegas, I met up with Beverly Griffin, cofounder of Griffin Investigations, the detective agency that's tracked card counters like Finkel for the past four decades. I got inside the surveillance room upstairs at the Bellagio to see how casinos track, videotape, and, they hope, win the cat-and-mouse game. Though it'd been years since they would have seen the mug of Jonny Magic on their screens, he was there in the database in case he ever tried to crush a blackjack table again.

That occasion arose soon enough. Part of the challenge of any story about cardplayers is verifying winnings. Outside of official tournament results, such as those maintained for Magic and World Series of Poker, players can easily exaggerate their methods or exploits. Throughout my research, I got multiple accounts of the stories and events reconstructed in this book. I learned quickly enough that Finkel isn't one to trump himself up; if anything, he's inclined toward modesty and self-deprecation. But to satisfy my journalistic inquiry, he showed me his accounts filled with gambling winnings and met me in Atlantic City to show me how he counts cards.

It was a cold day in January 2005, and Finkel was in town to play in a World Series of Poker event at Harrah's. "The last time I was here I was getting thrown out," he said, walking in. By the end of the night, he had stormed the first of two final tables that weekend—and was heading for his most lucrative week ever. As we headed for the blackjack tables after midnight, he was about to win even more.

As it turned out, some of his old card-counting buddies were also in town for the poker tournament, and they were willing to lend a hand. As my friend Mark and I stood watching, Finkel and the Lawyers reprised their old tricks, lingering around a table until the count got positive enough to jump in. Ninety seconds later, Finkel was stuffing his $1,250 profit in his jeans—and, feeling some heat, headed coolly for the door.

Over at the Borgata, the demonstration continued, as Finkel loomed over the action and worked the tables. It's one thing to hear about card counting, and another to witness it—or try it—firsthand. My attempts at counting didn't go far, and only made me more impressed by Finkel's skill. As he stood up with another wad of cash, I said, "It's like having superpowers, isn't it?"

"Yeah," he said, relieved that he could still pull off his game after all these years off the circuit. "It's kind of like riding a bike at this point," he said, then disappeared eagerly back into the pit.

As Finkel worked the other tables, I fell into a conversation with one of the guys now running the Lawyers' team. As we talked, he kept looking over my shoulder at the pit boss, who was now whispering to another big guy in a suit. The Lawyer abruptly arched his brow and motioned for me to follow him. "Jon just gave me the signal to leave," he said, quickly fighting through the crowd. "I'm surprised he still remembers it after all this time."

Ducked behind a bar where a lounge band was torturing Madonna, Finkel's buddy grabbed his ringing cell phone. "Yeah," he muttered, "he's right here." Then he handed the phone to me.

"Hello?" I said, tentatively.

It was Finkel. "You're contaminated," he replied.

"I am? What does that mean?"

"The pit boss saw you talking to my friend. Now he thinks you're part of the team, too."

"They think I'm counting cards?"

"Yeah," Finkel said, "and if they see you with me, then I'm going to be contaminated here, too." Though Finkel was in the Griffin book, that didn't mean the staff recognized him yet tonight. "Right now, I'm still clean," he said, "and I'd like to keep it that way."

"I guess that means good-bye for now," I said.

"Yeah," he replied, with a laugh. "Your friend's waiting for you outside."

I left him to the tables and hit the road. "If I knew I was going to get contaminated," I told Mark, "I would have tried harder to win some cash."

ACKNOWLEDGMENTS

Thanks to: Jon Finkel, Richard Garfield, and everyone else I hung out with and interviewed for this book; Wizards of the Coast; Mark Rosewater of WotC for digging up Magic archives; my agent, Mary Ann Naples of the Creative Culture; Random House; my editor, Jon Karp; Jonathan Jao; my family and friends.

ABOUT THE TYPE

This book was set in Garamond
No. 3, a variation of the classic
Garamond typeface originally de-
signed by the Parisian type cutter
Claude Garamond (1480–1561).

Claude Garamond's distin-
guished romans and italics first appeared in *Opera Ciceronis* in 1543–
44. The Garamond types are clear,
open, and elegant.